What An Elf Would Do:

A Magical Guide to the Manners and Etiquette of the Faerie Folk

By The Silver Elves

ISBN-13: 978-1477548523

ISBN-10: 1477548521

Printed in the United States of America by CreateSpace

Dedication

This is dedicated to our son, Draco Windwalker, the Lord of the Wind, whom we raised to be very polite and who has been unfailingly courteous throughout his life. Thanks for being such a great son! Our jokes may not be funny, but you were kind enough to laugh at them.

"If you have nothing good to say... at least, say it politely."
Ancient Elfin Admonifion.

Table of Contents

When an elf speaks, sHe does not attempt to appear wise, rather sHe speaks the truth from hir heart as best sHe understands it while ever remembering the education, propensities, and terminology preferred by hir listener. Being enchanters, elves are ever, even in the simplest of interactions, weaving spells of delight and joy, hoping to bring a bit of light and often humor into the other's life. The goal of an elf is never to raise hirs'elf above others, but to find a level where they can meet as one. The elf always begins by assuming and treating others as equals, and always with respect. In some situations, the elf finds listening a more profound statement than anything sHe might say, and sHe is always there for and ever loyal to hir friends.

Chapter 1:

Skills That Every Elf Is Encouraged To Develop

*E*lves are often reticent about other people. Due to ages of having to hide our true s'elves, we elves have developed a fear of, and know there is a very real possibility of persecution, or scorn, or derision if we reveal ours'elves. We have learned to be cautious relative to those to whom we reveal the truth of our being. Yet, being magicians and enchanters, most elves are able to spark up a conversation with nearly anyone of any race, or societal class if need or circumstances demand. We've even been known at times to carry on long conversations with individuals with whom we share no common language at all except the language of a friendly smile and the music of intonation that our voice conveys.

Some cultures have a prohibition against speaking when one's mouth is full. Most elven cultures do not share this prohibition, however, the tendency for garbled speech, as well as the possibility of spraying food fragments about, does tend to limit us from doing so.

We elves nearly always speak from our hearts. We do not always think before we speak, but that is not to say we are thoughtless in our speech. Rather, having developed ours'elves as souls and spirits we trust that whatever we say will be the right and appropriate thing to say at that time and for the particular company and circumstance. On the other hand, if we should make a social gaffe we are not overly dismayed for we are also experts at talking our way out of anything. Again, the important thing is our underlying intent. Our intent is always one of healing, encouragement, and positive connection. We always have an eye to the future, and we never speak without purpose, although sometimes that purpose is to charm or enchant our listeners. We understand that the true message is seldom the content of what is being said, but the genuine feeling of relationship that prompts our saying it in the first place.

Elves are primarily great listeners. Even when we don't seem to be paying attention we are aware of everything going on in a conversation, including the subliminal clues, speech tones, facial responses, as well as environmental aspects of atmosphere and ambience that are taking place. We don't feel a compulsive need to express ours'elves, so we don't interrupt others with a determination to show how clever we are. Our goal is not to be clever, but to foster relationship, and to nurture the individuals with whom we are developing a relationship. However, there are times when we must simply cut someone off, usually because we have to leave, and we do this as politely as possible.

It may happen that someone treats us rudely, but elves seldom return rudeness in kind, rather we tend to return rudeness with kindness. Those who tend to be rude to us find this baffling, and their bafflement is our revenge. Their rudeness is sometimes calculated to get a response, thus to manipulate us by demeaning us and our heritage; but the response they receive is seldom the one they expected, and therefore since we don't reply as expected they don't know what to do, except sometimes attempt to insult us further, which proves equally dissatisfying for them. However, it must be remembered that among man, and some other races, insults are a cultural way of relating to each other. They sometimes refer to this strange (to the elves) social interaction as breaking each other's balls or capping on each other. They don't necessarily mean what they say, and they expect that we will respond in kind. However, while we elves do attempt to meet people on their own ground, so to speak, we find we cannot engage in one-up-man-ship or a game of supposedly witty cutting remarks. At the same time, it is good to remember that this is an accepted cultural interaction among their kind, and while we don't participate in such demeaning behavior, neither do we criticize it or comment upon it in their presence.

If the waters of the great mountain
were to trickle down,
there would be no great ocean.

While elves tend to be very observant, and among ours'elves and in private we often discuss people we've encountered, and our observations of them and their behaviors, we try to bring insight, compassion and empathy into all our observations, and endeavor to not judge people, but rather to understand them so we may encourage them more effectively in future encounters. We almost never publicly admonish people, and while sometimes an individual's behavior leads us to withdraw from hir, or avoid hir company in the future, we always leave this individual with a blessing that sHe will find a better and more successful path as sHe proceeds with hir life, somewhere far from us.

Elves almost never argue. We don't argue with each other. We don't argue with others. Elves express our opinions as clearly and as succinctly as possible, and listen to the opinions of others with open minds and hearts. We consider what others say sincerely, and if we find they have a good point we alter our own opinions to incorporate that point of view. If we think their opinions are not valid we will offer our reasoning, and reasons/facts, as to why we think this is so. However, if they do not accept our reasoning and merely repeat their opinions, or as often happens when confronted by superior reasoning they no longer wish to talk about it, we also no longer pursue that topic. Having said what we believe, and having listened carefully, there is nothing more to say.

When we elves hear that friends are going to be married we always put a blessing upon them so that their marriage will be successful as long as it lasts, and that if it doesn't last they will part and ever remain friends. Friendship, to the elven way of seeing things, is the basis of all successful relationships.

Elves are enchanters and we love eloquent speech, yet in conversation our intention is ever affinity, positive relationship with the other, and clarity of communication, therefore we never put on airs or try to make ours'elves seem greater than we are. In fact, most often elves are very modest, and downplay both our powers and our regal heritage, almost never mentioning our titles, except where that is the topic of conversation, or the degree of our magical adeptship.

In general we elves do not correct other's errors of speech, grammar or pronunciations save in those instances, which are often quite common, in which our friends from other countries have asked us to help them improve their English (or whatever language the elf speaks). On the other hand, if we make an error of speech, or a mistake concerning some fact and someone corrects us, we always genuinely thank them for we are ever grateful for enlightenment.

Since we often get to know other folks from different cultures and language groups we frequently learn at least a few words of their language; at least enough to say hello, goodbye, and thank you, although many elves are polyglots and learn much more than that.

The Silver Elves

We elves are continually attempting to better ours'elves, our knowledge and our vocabulary, and among ours'elves we may use new words or concepts frequently until we have mastered their use and meaning. However, as ever, our communications are nearly always conveyed at the level of the person with whom we are communicating, for we never wish to make ours'elves appear inaccessible, or put ours'elves above others. We consider it rude to flaunt one's superiority. And in fact, from an elven point of view, making an issue of one's superiority is a very inferior thing to do.

❧

Elves tend to speak very simply and directly. We admire eloquent speech but for us eloquent speech is also the most direct and clear expression of our intent. As scientists apply the principles of Occam's Razor to their theory, so do we elves apply it to our communications. We never use flowery speech for the sake of sounding educated. It is always harmonious understanding that we wish to achieve with others.

❧

When listening to others, we don't merely bide our time until they shut up and we get to talk again. We actually listen to what they have to say and endeavor to understand it and to integrate it into our greater understanding of them as individuals and our comprehension of life in general.

❧

Failure cannot find those who never give up.

While elves can ask other elves nearly anything, it is important to remember that men and women of other races are often very touchy or sensitive about things and can, and do, take offense very easily. Thus it is not wise to ask a woman of another magical race if she is pregnant for she may in fact be overweight, or she may have had miscarriages previously and be worried about that, and thus sensitive to any mention of her pregnancy. You never know with these people, therefore it is best to always be careful in one's speech around them. Remember normal (non-faerie) women tend to be paranoid, and normal men tend to be grumpy. They can also take offense if you ask their age, how they are doing at work, or damn near anything. Did we mention these people are very sensitive and touchy?

We elves almost never raise our voices. When we get angry, which is seldom, we tend to lower our voices or become silent. None-the-less, we have found that normal folk often relate, not to reality, but to their expectations. Thus we have at times been accused of yelling at someone when we have not raised our voices at all, in fact, it is the other person who is yelling. This is because they feel we are yelling at them, even though we're not, or they expected us to yell, for that is what most people would do in the situation and thus they respond to what they thought would happen instead of what really is going on. They will also relate to an elf, and each other, based on past experience, which is to say if you remind them of someone they've known in the past, they will like you or dislike you based on their experience with that individual. It is irrational, of course, but it is good to remember that while we elves are a very reasonable and rational folk, not all people are.

Elves often apologize even when they have done nothing wrong. It costs us nothing and it often soothes the feelings of others. We always assume the responsibility for making things go well in our interactions with others, no matter what their behavior is. We are ever striving to develop within ours'elves the capacity for successfully handling any and every interaction no matter how recalcitrant the other person may be.

Elves do not tend to respond to life's uncomfortable or awkward moments with pat phases. In fact, we don't usually use common phrases at all. If someone has died we don't say to their loved ones, "I'm sorry for your loss," for that is what everyone says, and it sounds routine, hollow and meaningless to our ears. This is particularly true if we didn't actually know the person in the first place. In such circumstances, if we can't think of something original and genuine to say, we find it better to remain silent. Feelings are often better expressed without words.

When we are at home together, elves do whatever creative endeavors we individually or collectively choose. However, when we have company, we generally give our full attention to those who are visiting. If in the course of time you visit elves and they no longer spend a great deal of time visiting with you and instead go off to read, write, paint or whatever, you should be flattered, for it means you have been accepted as one of the family.

While we are cautious in what we ask others, we elves are not offended by questions, no matter what they may be. If someone asks us something that we do not wish to reveal, we may simply inform them it is private, although we tend to be more inclined to answer the question truthfully but without actually revealing anything, or we may, depending on the circumstances, answer in a humorous fashion. Among our own kind there is little that elves consider private, including our sex lives, and we will talk about nearly anything openly and frankly. Sometimes those, who are not elves, will ask a question for the purpose of being rude, but we seldom take offense. If the question can actually be answered we will respond to it, if it requires no response we may simply ignore it. In most cases, we do not respond to it in kind, although in some circumstances, with certain people we may do so, for some individuals need to know we will not put up with their bullshit. The question they were really asking was, Will you take it or not? The answer is, No. However, even under such circumstances we are not offended, nor do we speak in anger. And we have found that for many people, particularly males of mankind, this firm response is appreciated by them and they then accept us as equals. They want to know that we are not, in their terminology, a bunch of pussies. For the record, neither male nor female elves are individuals that one may trifle with, and go on one's way unscathed.

The elves say the best way to "save the day"
is to party till dawn.

When elves make appointments we keep them. However, if we can't we always let our host know at the earliest possible opportunity and explain why we cannot meet with them or keep a date. We usually do this in the most loving and kind way possible, expressing our regret. Usually we tell the truth as to why our plans have been changed, but some individuals, who are not elven, are easily offended so for them we make up something plausible that they can understand and accept.

૨૦

Elves often receive more than one invitation at a time. When we do we accept the one we feel most likely to be a good time. If more than one engagement seems inviting, we may go from one to another in a sort of Faerie Rade (Parade) recruiting more members to our party as we travel from place to place.

૨૦

Among other folk we elves almost never discuss religion or politics. We have our opinions, they have theirs, and people only get excited and get their feeling hurt if we don't agree with them, therefore, particularly while we eat we avoid such topics, preferring light and enjoyable banter about death or other amusing subjects.

૨૦

When dealing with unreasonable folks elves give up trying to reason with them, for that is useless, neither do we argue with them, for that is endless, instead we withdraw with as much courtesy as possible eager to be on our way to more convivial company.

૨૦

Elves ever attempt to bring clarity to relationships and situations. If someone expresses doubts about how someone feels about them, we let them know the positive things the other has said about them. We find most social conflicts between individuals are really misunderstandings that we do all we are able to do to clear up.

❧

Elves never carry rumors from one individual to another to cause further disharmony between them. That is a dark fey trick that we never indulge in. If someone says something negative about someone else we try to illuminate that other's motivations with compassionate understanding. While we may listen to someone's complaints about another we never join in, unless we are among our own kind and then we examine the individual with dispassionate analysis.

❧

Elves do not pile on some poor unfortunate that some person or in-group has decided to harass because they seem weak or an easy target. We do not need to demean others to make ours'elves feel powerful. We are powerful. We do not need to demean others to separate ours'elves from them in order to be in the in-group. We are the ultimate in-group. Others are lucky to be with us, and all sincere individuals who approach us with genuine intention of friendship are welcome.

❧

In looking at others, elves do not assume other people are ignorant simply because they do not know the things we know.

❧

We elves do not pretend to knowledge we do not have. We are rather eager and perpetual students of everything that catches our interest. We do, however, frequently pretend to be less knowledgeable than we actually are, less aware of what may be going on, and less astute about an individual's behavior, for there is much that can be learned in this way. Mostly though, we remain silent and allow people to assume whatever they wish about us and simply make no effort to correct them.

In dealing with others, we frequently ask for their opinions and observations for alternate and unique points of view are fascinating to us. However, among the normal folk it should be noted that their opinions are primarily a reflection of what they've recently seen on television, heard in church, or read in a magazine. Still, we listen carefully for this gives us an idea of the milieu of their societal sub-group.

While others often judge us by the standards of their particular ethnic, religious, or social group, we elves endeavor not to judge others by ours. Rather we attempt to understand individuals by how closely they adhere to, and are consistent with, their own beliefs and proclamations, which is also how we judge ours'elves.

Elves equate rudeness with ignorance, lack of education, weakness of character, lack of good breeding and poor social upbringing. Thus we strive to be polite even in the face of rudeness.

Particularly when we hold a position of power over someone, as is often the case with children, waitresses or other hired help, we are invariably polite in dealing with them. In fact, elves feel that such relationships demand an even greater attention to courtesy. Even when we are lords, which is the case with most elves since we come from a royal race and every elf is considered royalty, we do not lord it over others.

For the most part, elves are very modest about what we have accomplished. We prefer to leave others to point out and praise the things we've done and we, in turn, spend our time praising the efforts, no matter how modest they may seem, of those we encounter. It is a policy of the elves that all who encounter us will go away encouraged and feeling better about their lives and their own capabilities.

Elves don't tend to talk about ours'elves unless asked to do so; we prefer to inquire about the lives of others. This not only gives us insight into their character but also makes them feel that they are important to us, which they are.

Elves never tell others when they've failed to heed our advice and wound up making a terrible mistake, "We told you so," we just smile and know that that's what they're thinking anyway so it doesn't need to be said.

If someone rejects you, thank them.
They have helped you more than you realize.

If we are wrong, we apologize. If we are mistaken, we clarify our thoughts and opinions. If we have misspoken we correct ours'elves. In this way we ever improve our understanding, our knowledge, our relationships, and our own character and thus become ever more powerful.

❧

When others apologize to us, we accept their apology graciously, easing the task for them and often helping to bring sympathetic understanding to their error.

❧

For the most part, we elves do not flatter others. Yet, we are great admirers of other folk and their abilities and often compliment them on their dress, ideas, or any other aspect of thems'elves that we found particularly delightful. We are always sincere in our compliments, at the same time, it should be said we elves are also easy to please.

❧

If we have to chastise someone, we often do this in a roundabout way, so they will get the message without having to take it personally. We also do it with the greatest of good will toward them and a genuine intention of helping them and the relationship that exists or is developing between us.

❧

Relationship to elves is of vital importance and central to our culture, thus we are ever aware of the importance of introducing one set of friends when we encounter another set, thus bringing them each closer to each other and all closer to us. In the elven mind, all opportunities stem from relationship.

❧

Elves are aware of the greeting forms, habits, and traditions of other cultures. When meeting each other we often touch our hands to our hearts. When meeting men we shake hands when that is the common greeting of their culture, or bow if that is their tradition, or sometimes both. If their tradition were to touch foreheads and noses, as it was in ancient Hawaii, we'd do that as well. We always adapt ours'elves to those with whom we interact.

While we love listening to rumors, we seldom spread them, rather we seek to know the truth about all things and we are well aware that certain petty sorcerers use rumors as a means of harming those they envy. On the other hand, we commonly spread good comments about others and tell individuals the good things someone has said about them often clarifying misunderstanding, or allaying doubt that would obstruct their relationship, by doing so.

We elves are aware that among the things the normal folk are sensitive concerning are bad breath and body odor, thus we are ever careful not to mention these things with them if we encounter them. We are ours'elves a very hygienic folk, however, if we should discover that one of our own has bad breath or body odor we take them aside to warn them about this, for elves are ever thankful for such help and are not insulted when someone is attempting to assist them.

Elves do not need a special occasion to dress up. We are the special occasion.

Elves are very aware of our appearance and the effect it has on others. However, we do not have dress codes or fashion codes as some cultures seem to have. Each elf dresses in the fashion that pleases them, or in some cases, pleases those they love, and we expect other elves to do the same. Thus in most groups of elves one may find an enormous variety of styles and fashion from old velvet and lace to casual t-shirt and torn jeans, and everything between and everything beyond.

Therefore, elves do not make fun of the fashions of others. Well, occasionally if it is something truly outrageous, like the time we saw a man dressed in an undershirt and a pain of boxers worn backwards so the flap would reveal his ass in the breeze. We did laugh at that, but only among ours'elves. We never criticize others about their style or attempt to make them feel uncomfortable. Again, we wear what we please and expect others to do the same.

Elves often carry a clean handkerchief around with us, and then we blow our nose and there you go. So if we encounter someone who needs a good cry we will cast about for some tissues, elfin females sometimes carry them, or some other item for them to cry on, or we will even offer our shoulder to cry on it there is nothing else. As far as blowing their nose, we will do our best to help them, but really they should be carrying around their own handkerchief or tissues.

While many cultures have prohibitions concerning public nudity, and elves observe these restrictions when we are among those cultures, we do not share them and among ours'elves elves often go about nude or half clothed and none of us think anything of it.

The very first magic words each elf learns are Please and Thank You. These are simple words but their magical power is tremendous and the spells and formulas that surround them have ages of use empowering them. It is true we have developed more complex and sometimes more eloquent enchantments but these simple words of power never lose their potency, particularly when used with genuine intention. As nearly all elves know, courtesy is the underlying power of enchantment and our advanced enchanters have refined this power into a social dance of great elegance and beauty. Elves use these magical words frequently, and we never fail to give thanks to those who have aided us in any fashion.

While we elves are often thought of as party animals, the truth is that duty is always foremost in our minds and hearts. Therefore, when we are asked to participate in some potentially pleasant experience or gathering, we always ask ours'elves first where our duty lies, and if the event does not conflict with our duty then we are usually eager to accept such invitations if at all possible. Even if we cannot go we always express to our potential hosts how much we would have loved to participate, our explanation for why we are prevented from doing so, and how much we hope that even though we cannot accept this particular invitation that they will remember us in the future.

When someone tells us, "no", we accept it. To do otherwise, to attempt to force our will upon them, is to evoke evil magics and therefore terrible karma, which we elves try never to do. The will of the individual in most cases is inviolate. There are naturally exceptions to all things. When a child in our care doesn't wish to do what is best for it, or wishes to do something we know to be harmful, we will intervene, although even in such cases we explain thoroughly why we are doing so, and why our intervention is necessary. However, even when someone says no, we are permitted to use our powers of enchantment and persuasion to change the individual's mind. We do not force our will upon them, but if they can be enticed or persuaded that is certainly fair. Naturally, we elves ever keep the individual's best interests in mind, like a good parent, and never persuade someone to do something that benefits us but harms them, or even what benefits us without profiting them in some way. We know that in a cosmic sense, they are us, that is to say they are a part of our world; and we'd no more harm one of our other's than we'd willingly cut off one of our toes if we didn't have to do so.

When we reveal we are elves, certain individuals are inclined to make callous, insulting remarks that they think are clever about our elven identity. For the most part we ignore these remarks, just as we are inclined to ignore ignorant comments concerning all manner of things. While occasionally a fool may say something wise, it is usually by accident and not to be counted upon.

Being magicians, wizards, sorcerers, shamans and other forms of magical folk, we elves know we learn more from listening than from talking. Thus we practice listening regularly. When legends speak of our pointed ears that is often just a metaphor for the fact that we listen very pointedly with true intention to understand. At the same time, we know that there are individuals who become uncomfortable if we don't speak, and even those who love to babble often require frequent reassurance that we are listening to them, which we give them to assuage their insecurities, or not if they are so irritating that we wish them to babble elsewhere.

We elves don't waste our breath attempting to express our opinions to those we know will not listen with an open mind for we will only be obliged thereby to listen to their inane rants for Elfin knows how long. Only where it is a matter of life or death, or where the Magic requires it will we express ours'elves to such individuals, not because they will necessarily listen to us, even in such significant moments, but because the Magic requires that they be warned. If they ignore us, that is their folly.

We elves tend to make all things pleasant as much as possible, combining work and pleasure on a regular basis; however, we are aware that others may despise their work, or simply wish to get away from it, and so we always allow others to guide us in conversation, choosing the topic as they will, and if they do not wish to speak of work, or their personal life or history, we do not press them to do so.

Certain individuals love to talk to elves, lecturing us on this and that as though we were ignorant. These boorish individuals have no realization of how boring they actually are, and we do not tell them; but we do tend, as much as possible, to avoid their company in the future. We elves are not fond of being bored, particularly when the boredom is forced upon us.

੪

If our elven kin make a social gaffe, we never correct them in public, preferring to use our own behavior as an example. The same if true if they misuse a word, we will simply use the word ours'elves in the correct fashion as unobtrusively as possible. However, in private we may have a quiet word with them in order to clue them in. Elves are always thankful for such help.

੪

Being magicians we prefer to promote change though action rather than words, however, we are aware that the need for significant changes must be thoroughly explained and justified before we attempt to get others to assist us. Therefore, when we propose to make changes that may affect others we lay the groundwork by going over what we intend to do, and the effects that will occur by our doing so, a number of times before we initiate any action. This preparation for action helps ease the way.

੪

Elves know how to change the topic if needed without appearing to do so. If we need, or decide to depart we can do so quickly and effortlessly without long explanations, or goodbyes, unless indeed we wish to linger and only have to go out of need, then quick goodbyes will be followed later by more lengthy explanations.

੪

We elves do not tease each other as we've seen other peoples do who seem to think "busting each other's balls" an amusing pastime, or who practice cutting each other down as a form of social interaction. We know that even though they pretend they are not offended by such things, their feelings are often hurt deeply, and their "capping" on each other frequently leads in time to violence, or at the very least to irreparable feelings of distaste and hate for each other. We've observed that among certain races their "comedies" consist almost entirely of people making hurtful but supposedly witty comments about each other. Elves do not find such things amusing.

As twilight ascends,
we gather close,
our desire keeping rhythm
to the drum beats

of our hearts,

our elf eyes aglow
with the expectation

of what is
in our minds already reality.

Chapter 2 :

Among the Masses

When elves ask someone how they are doing, we are genuinely inquiring into their welfare. Most folks simply reply, "Fine," or, "Good, how are you?", etc. but we do not mind if people actually tell us their problems. Often it happens that we have no material power to help them. If we can be of assistance, we will help. Although we are not entirely "soft touches" and do not give beyond what we can afford to give or do. If we cannot help the person in a material way we, none-the-less, will assist them magically if we feel they need our help by evoking or creating elementals that we send to assist them.

On the other hand, when people ask how we are doing, we understand that this is merely a social greeting and unless they indicate a genuine interest in our affairs we do not share our personal struggles with them. And honestly, we elves are for the most part extremely lucky folk, and most of the time our lives are going very well, and when we do have problems we know that there is little most others can do about it. So we do not involve them in worrying about our difficulties, which does neither of us any good.

We elves also understand that while we are indeed blessed and very lucky folk, most people who inquire about our day don't want to hear about how great we are doing other than a simple, "Very well, thank you." We consider it rude to rub our blessings into other people's faces.

❧

Also, we elves are a very creative folk and generally have a number of projects going in art, music, writing, etc. However, once again, when people ask how we are doing, they don't want a list of all our projects unless they specifically ask, and for the most part, we are not inclined to tell them since we'd rather be working on our projects anyway.

❧

When elves encounter an acquaintance who has gained a lot of weight or has undergone some other radical change in appearance since we last saw them, we don't say, "Jesus Christ, you've gotten fat!" although we may think it, and say it among ours'elves. Rather, we demonstrate how very glad we are to see them again, and politely inquire into their wellbeing. If they wish to tell us about the changes they have undergone, we know they will volunteer that information without us inquiring. In fact, it is our open acceptance of them as individuals that will most likely prompt their revelation.

❧

Old Elfin saying:
We'd never lie to you.
Except for your own good.

Elves are aware that people are likely to resist change when they feel criticized. They are more likely to initiate change when they feel supported for who they are as individuals, and empowered to make their own decisions. We elves always hope for, and support positive change in those we encounter, thus we encourage them at whatever stage they currently find thems'elves, and support the positive aspects of whatever situation or circumstance they may be in. It is this encouragement that often gives them the psychological will power to make positive transformations.

❧

When a friend comes to the elves asking advice about making changes in hir life, we give that advice in the most practical way possible. We do not make moral judgments, or give advice based on our personal spiritual philosophies, unless specifically asked to do so. We listen and give what advice we can based on our experience and knowledge of the world, and our understanding of the abilities and intellect of the person inquiring. We do not judge them; however, we always have our friend's best interest in mind, and consider their soulful, by which we mean their feelings about thems'elves and others, and their spiritual development, by which we mean the courage with which they encounter the world, as well as what is best for their physical body, which is to say their health.

❧

One doesn't become an elf simply because they've blundered into Faerie. But wherever we elves go, Elfin swirls around us... like the Mist coming from the sea.

35

Sometimes a friend will come to us who has made some radical change in appearance, fashion, or even had cosmetic surgery. Elves know that physical appearance, like so many other things in life, is a matter of taste and so we seldom comment upon the change except to say how good they look. If they have any doubts about their new look, they will express them. If they don't, there is no sense in us expressing a view that is only an opinion anyway, and will probably only serve to create distance between us. One can only influence those who are close to one, and we are less interested in what a person wears or looks like than how we feel about each other. Therefore, we support our friends in all the positive changes they make, and if the change they make is a superficial one, as fashion tends to be, we support that as well, for it really doesn't matter what they wear, but it is vital that they are happy about wearing it.

When elves encounter a friend who has undergone a change of faith or religion, we support them in this change. If they have taken on a new name, as often happens, we use that name for them. If they talk to us feverishly about their new revelation, which frequently occurs when someone has taken on a new faith, we listen politely. We may ask relevant, but non-judgmental, questions about what they are telling us. We are unlikely to follow them into their new faith, and it is possible, even likely they will abandon us to spend more time with those who share their new faith; but we want them to know inwardly that if they ever move beyond it, or wish to see us again, we will always be there for them. We are elves and we are ever loyal to our friends.

Elves have a basic policy concerning names. People can either call us whatever they wish to call us, and we will do the same with them; or they can call us what we wish to be called and we will also respond in kind. People usually find the second option more pleasing.

&

We elves approach all individuals as equals. If we are among royalty or others who use their titles, we feel free to use our titles as well. But if we are among ordinary people, we come to them as ordinary elves, the wee folk, and use no titles for these folk. We never wish to appear above folk, but are always one with them.

&

Unless people ask for our opinions and advice on how they may improve their lives, we elves keep quiet and mind our own business. In our experience, those who go around telling people what they should do, even when they are sincerely trying to help, usually are covering up the fact that they own lives are a mess, and thus they try to interfere in everyone else's life so they won't have to deal with the frustrating reality of their own. As an aside, they also tend to move their furniture around frequently, or make other superficial changes in their lives, always trying to change the outer world instead of dealing with their inner world.

&

There are no exceptions to

the rules in Elfin,

there are also

no rules..

When we elves encounter a friend who is clearly suffering from some illness or disease, we surreptitiously send them healing energy. We may ask them a few simple questions to understand what they are dealing with and how to best help them heal. We may tell them that we are sending them healing energy, but often this just gets in the way of the healing. It is said that one should not, or can not, heal someone without their permission, but the permission we deal with is an inner understanding and if they do not really wish to heal, or are karmically prevented from doing so, we know our healing will not take effect. Otherwise, all individuals wish to heal. It is part of the life urge, the drive toward immortality that is one of the primary goals of all life, so we don't really need to ask if someone wants to go on living. They almost always do.

❧

Sometimes someone comes and lectures us without us asking them to do so about things we know ever better than they do. However, we usually don't reveal our superior knowledge of the subject, we simply listen, for to us they are like students demonstrating their knowledge in front of their instructor. And by listening to them, we seek to teach them something as well, by virtue of our example.

❧

We elfin always approach life with a certain humility for we have discovered that it is a lesson life teaches whether one wishes to learn it or not.

At times, an individual, we use that term loosely in reference to these sorts, will come to us bragging about how great they are at this or that, or all they plan to accomplish and the great achievements they will be obtaining and accomplishing in the future. As ever, we listen with polite understanding. We do not see this as bragging, as most people would, or as they tend to do when they encounter this in others, but rather we see it as these individuals expressing what is truly their aspiration. We know that it is quite possible, perhaps even likely that they will never reach the heights to which they aspire, but that doesn't bother us either. We do not discourage them, nor do we, unless specifically asked, list the numerous obstacles they face in attempting to ascend to such great heights. Nor do we point out how utterly ridiculous their aspirations seem in light of reality. Nor that we think they are living in a fantasy world detached from practical reality. We see it as our duty to encourage them, for without encouragement how will they obtain anything? And who are we to say what individuals are really capable of achieving when someone bothers to believe in them? And even if their aspiration seems unlikely, even impossible, to be fulfilled in this lifetime, we know that there are lifetimes still to come and we elves act not just for this life, but for future lives as well.

ॐ

Sometimes folks approach the elfin as though we know the answers to all of life's questions. We surely do not. Infact, we very much doubt that we know all the questions.

It is important for elves to remember that nearly everyone we encounter, whatever the age of their bodies, or ours, is younger than we are in terms of soulful and evolutionary development. Thus it is important to understand their behavior in light of their youthful nature. To us, nearly all people are actually children and should be given compassionate understanding in light of that fact. And for those who are truly, soulfully, older than we, we find they are often very child-like as well. In Faerie, we are all really children.

We elves often encounter Mr. Know-it-alls who are filled with facts and opinions on every subject, and present themselves as knowing something about everything even concerning, sometimes particularly having to do with, the most trivial of topics. While we don't always believe them, none-the-less we listen to them with detached air for one can learn many things, or even be inspired by those whose principle goal in life seems to be to bore us to death. Still, any information we do receive from them we cross check with more reliable sources, although most of what they tell us isn't even worth remembering.

Even when people tell us what sounds like the most incredible gibberish that makes absolutely no sense in terms of normal reality, we listen carefully, perhaps even more carefully, for what seems nonsense to most people often reveals a spiritual, magical and/or psychological truth about someone to the elves. Plus, the spirit often speaks through those who seem insane.

What An Elf Would Do

When elves encounter people who are in a hurry, we let them go ahead of us, if at all possible. If we are in a hurry, which is seldom, and somewhat contrary to our natures, we do not expect people to get out of our way. Instead, we calm ours'elves and allow the spirits to open the way for us. If we need to we will say, "Excuse me," excessively with nods and smiles as we make our way through crowds and trust in our magic to get us to where we need to be at the right time.

Even if elves are in a hurry, we don't push people out of our way, or deal with them brusquely. This is rude, not to mention somewhat dangerous when dealing with a world filled with the violent, the macho, and the easily offended. However, even if we were all experts in martial arts, we still would deal with people in this way. In fact, we would feel an even greater responsibility to be gentle and considerate of them.

We elves usually speak rather softly. We do not attempt to talk over people. Yet, we have noticed that certain people, usually of meager education, or raised in the lower social classes, often talk in loud voices, even when they are not angry or shouting. We don't know if they have lost some of their hearing due to listening to loud music, or they hope that even strangers around them will listen in, and be impressed by what they have to say. We, however, do not raise our voices to match their volume but continue to speak in the fluid, melodious and moderated tones that suit our nature.

When someone of a different gender than the one we may be attracted toward gives us a compliment, saying, "Hey, beautiful," or "Hey, handsome," we are not offended. We accept their compliment with the generous spirit that prompted it and most often return it with equal courtesy. It doesn't matter that they hold no sexual attraction for us. Appreciation merits reward in kind and we give it.

৵

Elves, for the most part, don't go around telling miscellaneous people that we are elves. This is not only because they tend to disbelieve us, even to make presumptuous jokes about our view of ours'elves; but also due to the fact that most folks are simply unready and unprepared for the truth. Thus we often introduce the fact of our elven natures in the lightest of ways, almost as if we are joking, so they may take it that way if they choose, while we gage their reaction, and decide therefrom whether to reveal more or to withdraw.

৵

When elves encounter the disabled or disfigured in the public, we neither stare nor avoid their gaze. It is a difficult situation. Sometimes they are offended if you stare at them, but they may also be offended if you don't look at them. It seems an impossible situation where you are damned if you do and damned if you don't. In general, we treat them like all other strangers. We may glance at them but do not stare. We do not avoid their gaze, however, and if they look at us we will look back. It is as simple as that.

৵

In cases when an elf encounters a friend who has been disfigured, we always look them in their eyes. We look directly into their souls and do not bother seeing the physical body except as the illusion it really is.

42

Elves know that when we look into people's eyes we are truly looking into their souls. We also know that if you gaze into their soul you open your own soul for their gaze. There is simply no way around this. The truer we become to our own s'elves and our true elven nature, the easier such gazing becomes.

We elves are aware that in the general public there are many who are made uneasy if you look into their eyes and they will turn away. We always turn away immediately after they do. It is the only polite thing to do and it is also the thing most likely to draw their gaze back to us.

Elves are also aware that among the various races (orcs, grimlens, men, etc.) there are those who believe that looking into their eyes is a challenge. It is like staring at a lion or some other wild animal. We elves never involve ours'elves in a stare down with such people unless we have come to the point where we are prepared to fight them to the death. This is not only because we are not inclined to engage in combat purposelessly, but because it is a violation of their social mores, and we never wish to violate other folks social customs unless we are impelled by necessity to do so. Of course, this often leads them to conclude we are weaker than they, and us to conclude we are more intelligent, wiser, and more courteous than they are, and they more primitive than us. Everyone has their opinions concerning others. We elves usually find it best to keep ours to ours'elves.

When elves are in the company or vicinity of those who are uncomfortable with us in any way, we often speak to their psyche, projecting our own thoughts to their minds, reassuring them that we are good folk and mean them no harm, or if we think they have hostile intent we let them know they are fooling with the wrong people and need to go elsewhere. Sometimes we will send short messages, such as, "It's okay," or "We're really your friends" in bursts using the light from our eyes and projecting it into their eyes in a flash. This usually makes them blink. However, we do not stare at them, for this would only make them more uncomfortable, but send the message quickly, and then turn away. We can do the same thing from the corner of our eye if we need to, so we don't seem to be looking at them at all, or more often to the corner of their eye when they are not looking or paying attention. If done over a period of time, people who have been shy of us, or seemed that they didn't like us for some reason because of some unnamed prejudice, will gradually become at ease with us, and even in time become very friendly.

છ

When elves encounter a friend we always make hir feel like sHe's a part of the family who has made hir way home after a long journey. This is true even if it has only been since yesterday that we last saw the individual. We are always delighted to see our friends and we always make it very clear to them that this is the case.

છ

"Proper technique can move mountains that power can not budge." Old Elfin Saying

Yet, we elves do not manipulate people. Manipulation is exhausting and usually not worth the effort. We do not try to force people to like us. We simply tell their unconscious the truth, which is that we are good folk and they'd be lucky to be our friends, more or less, although not necessarily in those words. Trying to force people to like or love you is a hopeless task, and one that is not worth undertaking. Or perhaps it is worth Undertaking to the point where it is finally buried for good. Rest its hungry ghost soul. Elves know that the very best and most powerful way to influence people is to be our own s'elves, and to be the best s'elves we can be consistently. Also, common courtesy is a magic that should never go unappreciated.

When elves encounter an acquaintance who has fallen on hard times, we do whatever is in our power to help them. Often, alas, that is little in terms of material support. But we will always bless them with some luck and a bit of magic to help them on their way. We only give advice if they specifically ask for it, and then very sparingly. We find that advice is usually the least effective means of helping someone, and seldom heeded anyway.

It is said that most woman love
a man in uniform.
Elves love an elf in costume.

The Silver Elves

When panhandlers approach us in the street, we elves give them a bit of money if we have it on hand, and to spare. The fact that they might use it for drugs or alcohol is not our concern. We are not in the business of judging the lives of others, or trying to guess whether someone will use the dollar or two we might give them well. That is their responsibility. Ours is to help as we can, where we can, and leave the rest to the magic. We've been genuinely blessed, and a dollar or two is but a humble means of sharing those blessings.

~

Sometimes when panhandlers approach us we give them a choice between a bit of money and our blessing. They always choose the money. This is unwise for they'd get a lot more out of our blessings, but that may be how they came to be in such a state in the first place. However, if they are particularly charming we will give them a blessing as well.

~

If a friend of ours has undergone, or is attempting a radical change in hir life to improve hirs'elf, we always support hir as best we can. It doesn't matter if the individual is trying to lose weight, give up smoking, give up alcohol, or whatever, we support hir efforts. It doesn't matter if sHe has undertaken this very effort a dozen times previously only to fail and fall back again into smoking or drinking. We support hir, because we know even if sHe gives up again sHe will eventually make the change she desires if sHe has our support. What is important is that we are there for hir, ever and always.

~

If a friend of ours decides to make a change in hir life that will lead hir away from us, such as a move across the country, we let hir know how much we will miss hir, yet we fully support hir in hir efforts to have a better life, have an exciting adventure, or whatever it is sHe is pursuing. We let them know that sHe will always be welcome among us even as we hug them goodbye.

When a friend gets involved with someone who is clearly wrong for hir, we do not warn hir against this other person. That is the most hopeless of actions and almost never turns out well. The friend will either fail to hear what we say or will turn against us. Instead, while in no way encouraging or discouraging the relationship, we reassure our friend that we support hir in all hir actions and we will always be there for hir.

If a friend gets involved with someone we cannot have around, we regretfully let our friend know that while we appreciate hir as a friend, we simply cannot be involved in anyway with the other person. We explain clearly why this is so and leave it at that. We do not ask the person to choose between us and hir new companion, but rather assume sHe will choose the other and bless hir on hir way. If our friend comes to hir senses and gives up the other on hir own, we rejoice and do our best to console hir and help hir find a better replacement for that relationship. But we do not interfere with the relationship itself, for if we did so the friend would always tend to blame us for its failure and we do not want that. Always, we support our friends' right to choose, whether they choose wisely or not in our view, does not matter as much as the fact that they have taken responsibility for their own lives.

We elves don't give our friends advice about relationship unless they specifically request it, and even then we are very cautious and circumspect because we know from experience that even when someone asks for advice they don't really want to hear something they haven't already decided upon thems'elves, and they are even more unlikely to follow our advice, even if they agree it is the most sensible thing to do.

❧

If friends of the elves get into a quarrel, or separate, or divorce, we do not attempt to get them back together; nor do we take sides. We support each of our friends in hir own efforts to pursue hir Will and Vision in life, while doing all we can to help our friends remain friends even if they do not get back together again.

❧

We elves are aware that many cultures take their sports very seriously. They are joyous, even insanely so, if their chosen team wins, and depressed unto despair when their team loses. This all seem slightly bonkers to us, but we don't point that out to them as they would either be offended, or offended and violent. At the very least, they could no more understand our lack of enthusiasm than we can understand their arbitrary passion for something that seems to us to be but a fleeting pastime. It is not that we elves don't ever follow sports, for many elves do, but for us the whole point is a good game well played, and to us that happens when both teams play their very best. The best games to us are usually closely matched and well played games. Therefore we encourage both sides to do their best and often root for both teams, since that is likely to turn out to produce the most interesting game, and we are always winners in the end.

On the other hand, as we say, we know how seriously other folk take their sports, so if their team wins, we congratulate them, and if it loses we commiserate with them, if called to do so, which usually we are not, but one never knows. We often find that saying such things as, "Great Game," or "Well played," are relatively safe to say. If someone disagrees with us, we just nod knowingly, as if they've said something sagely and profound that we've never thought of before even when their just say what seems to be a bunch of gibberish to us.

Some elves acquaint thems'elves with sports info, even if we have no interest in sports, just so we can pass among other folk seamlessly. Some of us, however, simply can't be bothered, could care less, and usually find it best just to keep our mouths shut, nodding if needed.

If someone comes up to us and asks, "what did you think of the game?", we don't usually lie and say, "It was amazing," if we haven't seen it, although we could. Nor do we ask, "What game?" usually. Often we say, "Oh, I missed it," as though we missed the birth of our first child, and, "How'd it turn out?" in case they are eager to tell us.

Some times someone will ask, "What do you think of ...." and we don't know if it is a sports figure, a movie actor, or a politician, and we don't want to tell them we have no idea, although we have done that very thing. We may say, "Not really sure, what do you think?" which is nearly always a safe question because they usually only mentioned the person in the first place so they could give us their opinion concerning them.

When a friend invites us to a sporting event, church event, or political rally or any other event that we don't have the slightest interest in, we elves don't tell them, "That sounds really boring," or even, "No way." We express our sincere sorrow at not being able to share with them and let them know we have some (any) prior commitment and will not be able to attend.

❧

Legends often say that we elves are unable to enter churches. It isn't actually true. We can enter churches if we choose; we just seldom do so. It is not churches that repel us but monotonous and boring preaching. However, if someone urges us to accept Jesus as our lord and savior, we usually find it easiest to simply tell them we love Jesus, which usually shuts them up. Of if they say, Praise Allah, we may say, "Oh, Allah is a great god. One of our favorites." Actually, that last is a joke and since many Moslems are Grimleans who tend to lack any sense of humor, we usually say, "Praise Allah," in response, which is generally satisfying to them. This is not to say that all Moslems are Grimleans, for that is not so, but we do find most of those we've encountered to be pretty serious about their religion and while we respect that, we also tend to avoid individuals who take their beliefs that seriously. Also, Grimleans tend toward fanatic aspects of every religious and political stripe and will eagerly argue with and even kill each other for their opposing beliefs. Tread lightly around them. Never openly make fun of their precious, and to them sacred, opinions. They can become very dangerous, even deadly if you do so.

❧

While in private we elves might laugh about the Morons, the Church of the Ladder Day Taints, the Bapcysts, the Cathoholics, the Seven-Day Inventists, Jehovah's Witless and other names of affection that we have for various religious groups and devotees, to their faces we are always polite and respectful of their religious beliefs. This is not only because they tend to be insane to the point of mania and violence about these things, insisting their God is a God of Love while they plummet us with words or fists, but principally because it is discourteous to be rude to them, and ruins any chance of a positive interaction in the future, or of us influencing them by example. It is true that these very same folk will make fun of our claim to be elves to our faces, but that does not mean we should stoop to their level, or demean ours'elves with petty spiteful responses, like children on a playground yelling, "You are," "No, you are," back and forth to each other. However, in private they are free to say whatever they wish about us, and we will surely do the same. On the other hand, if they actually think of something amusing to say about us, we're more likely to laugh than anyone.

Despite the above, to elves the most primitive way of criticizing individuals is to make fun of their names. Man and others do this frequently, most often when they disagree with someone, as though making a pun with someone's name actually constitutes rational argument. We do it just for the fun of it, and to show them that if it comes down to it, we can play the game their way and usually much better than they.

While elves don't hold much respect for individuals who preach one thing and do another, we none-the-less treat them respectfully, for how else are they to learn?

∂∾

Elves admire individuals who practice what they preach. We may not agree with what they preach, but we greatly admire their consistency of character, as long as they don't attempt to force their beliefs on us. If they do that, while we still might admire them for their consistency, we will, none-the-less, use our magic to slap them silly.

∂∾

When individuals try to sell us something we don't want, we will often tell them they are wasting their time. Despite this they often continue trying to sell us, and we may continue to listen to them letting them waste their time. We warned them after all. We don't tell them they are wasting our time, because they aren't. We are responsible for our own time and only we can waste it. If we don't wish to talk to them, we will thank them and depart. Nearly every elf knows how to quickly and easily extricate hirs'elf from an unwanted companion without the need for arguments or discourtesy.

∂∾

When we are visiting foreign places, we elves don't go on in public about how things are so much better where we are from, even if it's true, or even if we think no one around us understands our language. It is simply rude to do so. What we do is our best to make the most of the situation, enjoy it as best we can, learn all we can from and about it, and practice our various magical powers of courtesy, patience, endurance and tact in order to master the situation.

∂∾

Elves take the saying, "Be it ever so humble, there is no place like home," to heart. We know that while individuals from other countries and cultures don't always think highly of their leaders or their governments, they are almost inevitably fond of their country, their culture and their people, no matter how humble the circumstance from which they come. They are often quite sensitive about these things so elves are ever cautious concerning anything we might say about them.

We have however noticed that often these immigrants from other countries often complain about how much better things were in their country than in the one we are choosing to live in. We find it terribly inconsiderate and want to ask them, "Why don't you go back?" However, it would be rude, although justified for us to do this. And we know that really what they are saying is how much they love and miss their country, their people and their culture, and they would surely be there if it weren't for their government and their leaders. We cannot help but feel a certain sympathy for them, and it is this, primarily, that keeps us from telling them to, "scurry back to where you came from."

But we know as well that these folk often find themselves scorned and hated by those who hate everything that is foreign and different from them and so, if they let us, we befriend them, and make them welcome among us, and give little heed to their whining born of homesickness, and with tender consolation seek to learn of them and their culture, for that makes them feel most welcome of all.

And when we are among those who once were masters of a land, but are no more, having been supplanted by those who are more violent, aggressive, and materialistic, and who are now treated with distain and as second class citizens, we always treat them with respect as we do all people. We do not place ours'elves above them, or treat them with haughty contempt as we've seen so many do, or act as if our skin color, ethnicity, education or some other, usually accidental, feature of birth entitles us to treat them with scorn, or make rude demands of them. For such arrogant behavior is repellent to elves, and we know that in time it accumulates a terrible karma that will lay low those who indulge themselves in it.

We elves know ours'elves to be of noble blood and heritage, but we do not need others beneath us for that to be so. Nobility is principally a consequence of character and not of birth, and if there were none but the noble about us we would not be less noble but even more so. For nobility uplifts all who encounter it, and being among the truly noble helps us aspire to greater nobility of spirit ours'elves.

It's not so much that the blood of our ancestors flows in our veins, as the fact that we were our ancestors.

Chapter : 3

Romance and Courtship Among the Elves

When an elf is invited to a wedding where sHe has previously slept with the bride or groom or both, sHe doesn't mention this to the other guests, but celebrates the wedding as though two virgin star crossed lovers and soul mates have finally found each other and wish them each and both the greatest happiness.

Elves love weddings. Or actually wedding receptions, particularly if there is food, drink, dancing and a chance of romance involved. Therefore, we are always joyous to hear when a friend of ours is getting married.

When we elves give wedding gifts, unless it is something the couple has specifically asked for, we give them something that they can return and trade in for what they truly desire. We also put a blessing on the card we give with the gift, so whether they keep the gift or not, they and their union will be blest by us. That is our true gift.

We elves avoid drunks. We have no problem, usually, with drinking or even maintenance alcoholics, those that have to have a beer or two or a couple of glasses of wine everyday to maintain thems'elves, but don't usually get drunk. But drunks are another matter and they often let themselves go at wedding receptions, and other such events, and we do our best to steer clear of them. We do not chastise them, or try to sober them up; we simply do our best to stay out of their way. If they approach us at such gatherings, we tolerate them, but give them no energy, and calmly wait till we can politely extricate ours'elves from their company, or they see someone else more appealing to plague with their sloppy presence.

If an elf encounters an old love with a new flame, the elf always wishes them the best of luck together. Jealousy is seen by the elves as a weakness of character and we endeavor always to rid ours'elves of it. Friendship is the underlying principle of all elven relationships, so we ever try to promote it. To an elf, an old flame's new lover is potentially a new friend, and from friendship all opportunities arise, thus we are ever eager to make new friends and greet this new person warmly.

If an elf encounters an old love with another previous lover as hir new flame, the elf greets them both warmly. This is not directly an opportunity to make a new friend, but the renewal of old friendships itself bears many possibilities and should not be overlooked.

Elves consider it impolite to go on and on about how great one's ex-lover was, or how wonderful one's other lover is. Elves generally consider nearly every sexual encounter to be great, and we don't rate one against another. That's just rude. Our current lover is nearly always the greatest lover we've ever had, and will continue to be so until our next lover.

Elves sometimes get involved with those who are not elven and for whom jealousy and possessiveness are accounted not only Normal, but as virtues. These individuals seem to have a need to hate those they were with previously, but with whom they are no longer involved. This is sad to us, but in encountering such people with whom we were formally in a relationship, we always greet them with courtesy, if they will let us. And we endeavor to renew the friendship if possible, which it isn't always, because they just won't allow it to happen. For this reason elves become very careful about becoming involved romantically with individuals who are not spiritually developed, although it is sometimes hard at the outset to see how they will act when it ends. However, time and experience develops our far sight, Telpareon, and we come in time to recognize such individuals as soon as we meet them, and to eschew relationships that we recognize will not turn out well.

When elves divorce we always try to remain friends. We do this not just for the benefit of the children, if there are any, although this is a foremost consideration, but because this is the best and most courteous way to proceed in any situation and relationship, and ever leaves open the possibility of opportunities for connection for the future.

Children often come with second marriages, and we elves treat these additions to our family as our very own. In a certain sense, elves view all children as their responsibility, for we are a very community oriented folk. We do not call these new additions to our family stepchildren but consider them our own sons or daughters, for so they are to our minds and hearts.

≈

The wicked stepmother that is the theme of so many cultures, is not a myth, legend, or tale for elf folk, except as a warning about how other folk may be. A new elf mother is a new friend and we elves are always glad to have more friends.

≈

When an elf marries into an already existing family, sHe doesn't attempt to supplant the natural parent. In fact, we often don't try to be parents at all. We leave that to the genetic parents. We treat the children of our other as new friends, and leave the disciplining of them, if needed, to their natural parents. If we are called to discipline them, we do so by the guidelines of their natural parent. We do not try to impose our own theories of parenting upon them. It is the most hopeless of things to try to discipline another's child without that parent's agreement. The children won't stand for it, neither will their parent, and it will only create a wedge between them and us. Thus we elves resist the urge to think we know better than a child's natural parent on how to raise them. Or if we do we use persuasion to help that parent understand and positively consider what we think is a more effective way to rear children.

≈

Elves always endeavor to make friends with our new lover's ex, and make them feel welcome as friends in our relationship. This not only resolves a lot of tension, opens up new possibilities for us, but we also learn much about our current lover that we wouldn't know otherwise. And if we should eventually break up with our current love, it is always possible we have a friend for life in their ex.

&

If we part from a relationship we always attempt to remain friends with our ex and our ex's children. After all, we are likely to encounter each other again, particularly if we share the same circle of friends, or work together, and it is always best for us, them and society, when relationships proceed and evolve with love, friendship, and mutual respect and courtesy.

&

When elves enter a relationship we often come to agreements about how the relationship will proceed. If we agree to be faithful, we are, if we agree to an open relationship, we have that as well. If someone fails to keep their agreement, we may pull out of the relationship as a romance, but we will always try to remain friends.

&

Elves don't have a concept of cheating in relationship. Relationships are not a test, although they may seem to be to many folk. Relationships are an opportunity for intimacy. If the relationship doesn't work out as agreed, there is always the future. For to the elves every relationship is a learning experience. There are no arbitrary tests, and the only passing grades go to those who can maintain their friendship both during and after the romance.

&

We elves consider it rude to drool over other men or women when we are out with our others. We may glance surreptitiously, but ogling others is not elven, even when we are alone, and certainly not when we are with those with whom we are romantically involved.

❧

If elves find out that two of their friends are getting involved who are not really right for each other, we don't warn them to beware, or proclaim that their relationship is doomed. We promote what is best in the relationship, knowing it will probably end, but also knowing that they will get something out of it while they are in it, and that is what is truly important. When it is over we remain their friends, as always, and do all in our power to encourage them to remain friends with each other. While things may be a bit sensitive at first, particularly when one of them finds someone new before the other does, we do our best to help the other by introducing them around. We know that in time they will find someone else, and then they will find it much easier to be friends with their ex. There is nothing like a new relationship to bring clarity and understanding to an old one.

❧

Some folks claim the waters of Elfin are intoxicating. Others say it is the air or the fragrance of the flowers, the food, the drink... which is all true. But the most intoxicating thing about Elfin really, is the elves and the love we share.

When an elf is about to marry someone who isn't elven and we sense that this individual will turn the marriage into misery and eventually into a trauma-drama divorce, we may say, "Holy Shit, are you really thinking of marrying that crazy bitch or bastard? You do realize this person is a nutcase." And the elf will usually say something to the effect of "But I love her, him." And we may reply, "We hope that means you're having great sex because it's not going to be worth it otherwise, and even then, it will probably not turn out to be worth it for all the hell sHe will put you through." We may think such things, but isn't it rude to be so forthright with one's friends, even a close friend? What can we say, we're elves, and unlike many other races and the normal folk, we can be direct and honest with each other. It is true we might express our reservations about the relationship in a more diplomatic way, or with a bit more eloquence, but the result is the same. We're friends and it's our duty to let our friends know about potentials we see to which they are currently blind. And whether they listen to us or not, we will always be there for them. We're elves, we are loyal forever to those we love.

If a friend reveals to us that they are having an affair with someone other than hir bonded mate, we elves don't say, "How terrible," or, "You know this will not end well," or, "Someone is bound to get hurt," or, "How could you do that to so and so," or, "We knew this would happen eventually," or anything of the nature. What we do say is, "Give us all the juicy details!"

If a friend of the elves has just gotten out of a terrible relationship that we warned hir will end badly, we don't say, "We told you so." Well, we might, but only so sHe will listen to us more carefully the next time, and prevent future suffering. We know that individuals often tend to repeat relationships, constantly getting with those who are like the bitch or asshole they were with previously. Excuse us. Let us rephrase that: with the type of undeveloped soul who would only bring them down again. So, in this critical period when they are deeply feeling the loss of one such relationship, we try to gently teach them to shield thems'elves from such individuals, to recognize them when they encounter them, or if they can't recognize such individual their own s'elves, to trust us when we see them, and warn them about such Black Holes of misery and despair.

When we have a friend who is hopelessly in love with an energy vampire and they will not heed our warning, we do not go on and on trying to dissuade them. If it is their will to suffer, so be it. When they come to us after, we will nurture our friend as always, but if a friend does it too many times without listening to us, we will simply shrug and say, "But that's what you wanted." We do not chastise such friends. Or berate them. We point out the truth quite simply as always and leave them to figure it all out. If they are to be elven magicians, they must assume responsibility for their own actions and decisions.

If a friend comes to us and asks, "Should I get involved with so and so," we elves do not say, "Yes," or "No." Rather we point out the possibilities as we see them. The good points and the bad points and leave our friend to decide what to do. It is important to remember, life is ever unexpected and surprising. Humans may be predictable but Life for the most part isn't. Thus we advise our friends to make the most of any situation or relationship they may be in, accept what is good, change or leave what is bad, and always strive to make things better. Unless the person our friend is thinking of getting involved with is clearly and without a doubt an insane bastard or bitch and then we say, "Run".

When we elves are involved with more than one person, we don't compare them to each other, or set them against each other, nor encourage any jealousies or squabbling over us. Rather, we seek to harmonize our relationships, so each and all will be friends, for this is the only true way to create lasting and successful relationships. And in the elven heart, all relationships and loves, even if the romance has faded, should last forever.

When we elves encounter a friend who is out on the town, or having dinner with someone other than their usual companion, we do not rush off to the other to let hir know we have seen our friend with someone else. That is their business, not ours. We elves are not tattle-tales, in fact we despise tattle-tales, unless they are telling us something that is particularly amusing, interesting, or might be of some use to us.

We elves don't try to seduce individuals who are already in a committed relationship. That would just be rude. We always seek to support relationships that are working or improve, through our support and encouragement, those that aren't. We don't interfere with ongoing relationships, unless one of the parties is so unhappy that the relationship simply doesn't exist anymore except in appearance. That doesn't mean we might not flirt with them. We flirt with nearly everyone. That's just practice though, and we practice our enchantments endlessly to hone our skills. If we should succeed in enchanting someone who is in a committed relationship, we don't take advantage of it. We remind them of their commitment and await the future. We're not in a hurry, really. In an ultimate sense we have forever, and forever is exactly how long we wish all our friendships to last.

అ

When someone flirts with someone we love, and with whom we are in a relationship, we do not interfere. Our lover is free to do as sHe chooses. To stay with us, or go, as hir will directs. It is the most hopeless thing to try to force someone to be with you, or stay with you. Our lovers are with us because they wish to be. If they wish to depart they are free to do so, although surely we will miss them. Love cannot be compelled, or bought. Sometimes it can be earned, or won, but mostly it is the most precious gift that can be bestowed on one.

అ

With the right magic, every chill wind can be
transformed into a cool breeze.

If we elves encounter a friend who is having dinner, or is out on the town with someone other than hir usual mate, we greet them warmly, glad to see your old friend, and open to the possibility of a new friendship (should it happen that we don't already know the individual who sHe is accompanying). We may introduce ours'elves to hir companion if our friend, in hir excitement to see us, neglects to do so. We do not assume anything illicit is going on, since we elves don't really have the idea of illicit relationships in our culture. We may inquire about our friend's usual companion, but elves are always asking elves about other elves they know in common, or inquiring about those we may wish to know, and there is no harm in this.

We elves are baffled by normal human relationships. Often normals will get married and then they will "cheat" on each other. When the person gets caught "cheating", the other tells them they don't mind the cheating so much as the fact that the other lied to them. Yet, the other lied to them because sHe valued the relationship and knew that if hir companion knew about it, sHe would be angry, hurt, and/or break off the relationship. SHe lied to preserve the relationship when the truth would destroy it. Doesn't that mean they should keep the relationship? After all, they were perfectly, or more or less, happy when no one knew about the "cheating". How does any of this make sense? We elves find normals as mystifying as they surely find us. They regularly act unreasonably and illogically and seem to think this is a good thing.

When elves encounter normal folk, or have them as acquaintances, we've learned that attempting to reason with them, particularly about religion, politics, relationships, marriage, or child rearing, or nearly anything really, is near to impossible. Even when, for a brief moment, some of them may see the light and admit the logic and sense of what we tell them, their passions and prejudices, preferences and aversions, soon take over and they returned rapidly to their illogical notions and actions. What can we do but love them as friends, and treat them with as much compassion, courtesy, and kindness as we can as we shake our heads at their seemingly self imposed madness.

By the by, elves don't really have a concept of profanity. While we understand the power of cursing, that is putting a curse on someone, which we almost never do, since in our experience people most often curse themselves, we don't really have a concept of cussing. There are no prohibited words among elves. We can say whatever the fuck we want, and we do. However, we are also aware that among the general public there are many who have such prohibitions, so when in public we endeavor to curb our speech to reflect these individuals' prejudices, just as we don't tend to make love in public, or go around naked, which some elves might in our own society. On the other hand, elves love the creative and the eloquent, and while we don't have prohibited words, we do agree in part with those who observe that some folks use profanity simply as a substitute for increasing their vocabulary. This does not offend us, but neither does it appeal to us, unless used very creatively.

We elves are not offended by pornography as it is usually conceived by normal folk. Neither do we tend to watch it, except occasionally at fast motion, which can be somewhat amusing for a short time. We prefer our sex on film to be combined with great dialogue, a great story, performed by excellent actors, just as we prefer our sex in real life.

☙

Elves do not view sex or nudity per se as pornography, even if it is gratuitous sex, which we very much tend to enjoy. Elves see pornography as anything in which sex and violence/torture/force are committed upon an unwilling victim that promotes this combination in an arousing or gratuitous fashion. We find such things despicable.

☙

Most elves do not have prohibitions about talking about our sex life, or anyone else's. We do not, for the most part, consider these to be private things. They are simply events in our life and we are as willing to talk about our sexual experiences and encounters, or anyone else's, as we are a good movie, a well-written book, or a delicious meal, or some great adventure we have had, which usually is what sex is to us.

☙

While elves love to flirt, we do not tend to flirt, except in exceptional situations where this is deemed appropriate, when we are with our significant other(s). This would be considered rude unless indeed the flirting was intended to draw another person into an open relationship, and all individuals involved are okay with this. Under these circumstances flirting can be a very fun and an invigorating part of a multiple relationship.

☙

Elves are monogamous, polygamous, polygynous, polyandrous, and polyamorous. Elves are heterosexual, homosexual, bisexual, and pansexual if you include our willingness to sleep with aliens if they're charming enough. Get over it.

❧

Elven relationships are always consensual in our sexual and other relationships. Elves do not have sex, or even dinner with those who do not wish to have dinner with us. We do not force ours'elves on people or attempt to do so. We are enchanters. We get off by the fact that others want us. We are turned off by rejection and do not attempt to force people to like us, although we may continue to attempt to charm them if we encounter them again. But for the most part we do not waste our time trying to persuade others to like us when there are so many out there that do or will. Some people say, there are plenty of fish in the sea, we elves say, the forest is filled with elves, and almost all of us love to make love, love to flirt, and love romance.

❧

If a friend tells us they are using fertility drugs to try to have a baby, we say, "Oh, great, good luck with that." We don't say, "I always knew you were shooting blanks," or the numerous other things that some people regard as amusing or clever. Nor do we pry for details. If they wish to confide in us they will do so. Neither do we give them a lecture on adopting, childrearing, or the dangers of over population. If they haven't considered such things already, they are certainly not likely to do so because we mention them.

❧

If an acquaintance of the elves tells us they are using Viagra, Cialis, or some other Erectile Dysfunction Medication, we say, "Okay." We don't say, "I always knew you couldn't get it up, " or "You should try losing some weight, you fat bastard," or "You might be better off studying Tantric Yoga," though we may think such things, and wonder why they are telling us such a thing in the first place. Who runs around telling people that they can't get it up, or they are so lousy and inexperienced in love-making that they don't know how to keep it up for hours if circumstances call for it.

When a friend comes to the elves and tells us they are getting a divorce, we don't take sides, even if we don't know the other person. Our friends know we are always on their side. We do attempt to talk to them in such a way that they will make the transition as easily as possible and without undue conflict. That is always best for everyone in our opinion. We ever encourage a mature approach to the situation that will resolve the affair in the least amount of time with no lingering feelings of hate, vengeance, and personal suffering. Such things only prolong what is already over, and there is no point in that.

When a friend who has just come out of a divorce or a break up then comes to us and tells us they are about to get into another relationship essentially on the rebound, we say, "Go for it." We know it may not work out, but it often helps them move on from the previous relationship, and that is a good thing.

When a friend who has just come out of a break up or divorce comes up to us and reveals that they don't feel ready for a meaningful relationship anymore and think they will just go out and have a lot of meaningless sex, we say, "Good for you. Remember to use condoms."

We elves believe that whether a romance begins with an acquaintance, a friend, or a torrid affair with a stranger, it should always end the same way, as a friendship.

When we elves are apart for a long time, we trust our others to be faithful to our friendship. This does not mean they will not make other friends elsewhere, but that the friendship we have with them will ever endure. Friendship is something that is always better, as far as the elves are concerned, when there are more and more friends. The saying, the More the Merrier, is definitely an ancient elven saying. This, after all, is our plan for bringing peace to the world and success into each and everyone's life.

If a friend tell us sHe met someone through the Internet, or at a bar, or even a night class at the local college, we don't say, "Hope they're not a serial killer," although we do indeed have that hope. We also hope the individual will not turn out to be abusive, a heartbreaker, or any of the other numerous things we may encounter among those we haven't known very long, and don't know much about. Instead, we say, "Oh, great. Tell us all about it." Then we put a blessing on our friend for protection, love and success, and send hir on hir way.

When we elves have been invited on a blind date and we discover the individual that we are to escort is not our "type", we do not back out of the date. After all, we know we are merely meant to serve as a chaperone so that our friend's date will feel comfortable. It doesn't matter if we find our companion less than attractive, or intelligent, or whatever. We look upon it as an opportunity to both serve our friend and practice our skills of charm and enchantment. We deal with our blind date's soul, not hir physical, mental, or emotional form, and we do our best to make it the most enjoyable date sHe has ever experienced.

If we go on a blind date and our chosen companion for the evening clearly finds us less than attractive, we are not dismayed. We do our best to be a courteous and charming companion, and if sHe is not civilized enough to respond to this, that is hir problem. It also gives us a chance to practice our powers of enchantment, for romantic enchantment is often best practiced on those we know in advance will reject us. That way, we do not have to concern ours'elves with, will sHe say, "Yes," or "No," for we know the answer in advance, and can therefore relax and practice our wiles with confidence. Strangely, such confidence in ours'elves has its own magical effect on people.

We elves don't tend to argue with each other. Sometimes when we are stressed we get testy with each other, but we almost immediately recognize this fact and soon offer mutual apologies. Often we find ours'elves laughing at our s'elves even while we are feeling frustrated about something. Love and friendship are always our guiding lights, and courtesy and mutual respect our means of securing them.

We elves know that when people reject us it is usually because of their own uncertainty about thems'elves and how others will view them. We do not let this deter us. We act in a friendly way to all individuals, treating them with courtesy and respect, and those who are worthy of us will respond. The rest we bless upon their way, knowing ultimately that we are lucky to be rid of them. It is also our experience that really beautiful people are very strong and secure as individuals, and are most often kind to those who approach them. Even if they don't accept their advances, they reject them in such a way that one feels good about the experience anyway. Individuals who are not really confident about their beauty are often harsh, or even cruel in rejecting others, but that is due to their insecurity.

When we elves get angry with each other, we know some dark energy has penetrated our aura and as soon as we realize this, we immediately set to clearing the air between us, and banishing the circumstances that lead to this disagreement. It's not that we don't have differences of opinion, but it is important that these be expressed in a reasonable and civilized fashion. It is a terrible mistake to take disagreement with our ideas as a sign of personal disrespect, or a lack of appreciation for the value of our true natures. If disagreements are so powerful that we find we must go in different directions, we still endeavor to do so with love and friendship in our hearts, and a mutual appreciation for each other.

Chapter 4:

An Evening Out

When friends invite us out to dinner and ask where we'd like to eat we always inquire what sort of price range they are thinking of. We do not assume that we can go to the most expensive place about and order anything we wish, although that might prove to be the case; rather we always consider our friends and their lives and politely inquire about the flexibility of their budget. If we wish something more than we think they are able to offer, we urge them to let us help pay for the meal.

❧

If we invite friends out to dinner we ask them what appeals to them as they consider the menu, and if it isn't within our budget we politely let them know it is a bit beyond our means at that time. If they are elves or faerie folk, they will surely understand.

❧

We elves are very generous tippers. We always give at a higher rate than is considered customary. In this way we help Nature preserve the underlying balance that lives at the heart of the Universe.

❧

When we elves go out to eat with a friend that we know is less wealthy than we, we always try to pay for the meal ours'elves. If they insist on paying or paying their part, we relent and allow them to do so, for we would not wish to make them feel inadequate by doing otherwise. However, if we can we will convince them to let us pay for the meal and suggest they treat us to dessert or coffee somewhere else later.

It is seldom that we elves don't receive good service. In fact, usually the servers, hostess, waiters, or waitresses are too attentive. We are often tempted to tell them to go off and leave us alone for a while to eat, but we are too polite to just come out and say it. Instead we assure them that all is well, and we will call them when we need them. In the rare instances, when we don't receive the service we expect, we try to be understanding. Often people are overworked, or just having a hard day and we never wish to make it more difficult for them. Instead we offer them extra courtesy and consideration, which nearly always works to make their evening better, as well as ours.

For elves dinner out is not simply about the food, although the food is important. We also consider the ambience of the restaurant, both the décor and the feeling of acceptance and welcome, or lack there of, from the staff. But most of all the joy of being with our guests, if we happen to have some with us, and their satisfaction is most important to us.

જી

Sometimes, it may happen that our food has not been prepared correctly. This again, is very seldom, but it does happen occasionally, and when it does we simply inform our server, and invite them to try it themselves to understand what we find inedible about it. On the other hand, we elves are not picky people. We are not demanding. And we don't send food back simply because it is not perfectly to our taste. We leave that to disagreeable who think they are entitled for whatever reason to treat others shamefully. Elves, however, whatever transpires, never cause a scene. Public arguments are distasteful to us, and we never indulge in them. It is particularly beneath our dignity to argue with those whose duty, or job it is to serve us. If we do have a problem with a restaurant's service, we resolve it by speaking to the owner or manager, and if that doesn't bring satisfaction we simply withdraw our business and warn our friends of our experience there. Not to mention posting about it on the Internet to alert strangers who may be thinking about going there.

When we elves find a place we like to eat, we will go back regularly, establishing a relationship with the owners, managers, servers and even our fellow diners if we encounter any of these more than once and they respond to our smiles. We often develop new friends and contacts, thus opportunities in this way, and it makes for a more convivial evening. Also, when the servers, the cooks and the managers get to know us, and like us, and they almost always like us, we're elves after all, they often begin to bring us extras asking our opinion about this or that dish that they are thinking of adding to the menu.

If it should happen that our credit card is rejected, which has occurred to these elves because of the screw up on the part of the credit company, we simply pay in cash. We never go out to eat without sufficient cash to cover the meal if something should go amiss with our credit cards. Like the boy scouts, we always try to be prepared. We don't ask them to run it again, obviously they already ran the card and it didn't work. We certainly don't make a fuss about it, obviously it's not their fault, and really it has nothing to do with them. They are responsible for the food and the service, not for our credit cards functioning or not. Nor do we cuss the credit company, even though they are at fault. We may need to call them later to clear things up, but again that is not the business of the restaurant, our guests, or the other dinners. As nearly always, we are unflappable. We deal with the situation easily and without distress to ours'elves or anyone else. It is a minor issue anyway and best resolved through the technicians whose job it is to deal with such matters. We are not about to let such minor matters spoil a wonderful evening out with our friends.

When out to dinner with our friends we do not attempt to dominate the conversation. Rather, we allow them to guide the conversation as their hearts or minds prompt them, and we join in, adding relevant comments or data as we can. If there is something of importance to be discussed, we await the opportune moment to bring it up. Timing is usually very important in such matters, and as our mother often told us when we were young, it was wiser to ask our father for something we wanted him to agree to after he had his coffee in the morning than before, and after his dinner than when he was hungry. Often as our guest is enjoying a pleasant dessert, opportunity smiles upon us.

If we are out with friends and they wish to say grace before the meal, we say grace with them, particularly if they are footing the bill. It does not matter whether they wish to thank Jesus, or Buddha, or Allah and Mohamed, or the Great Mother for the meal, or any other person, spirit or demi-god. We are always thankful for a decent meal, and our thanks inwardly always go forth to The Magic from which all things spring. We are fully aware that different people have different ways of viewing the Universe, and we find it easy to translate their ideas into our own understanding of the true nature of Reality. Besides, if we say grace with them they then might spring for dessert as well. Although in our experience most folks who are so religious as to say grace in public tend to be cheapskates and are unlikely to do so. With such as these we're lucky if they don't ask us to go Dutch.

If we elves are out at dinner and a couple at another table get into an argument, we don't look at them directly, since often even though they are making a spectacle of themselves, they may take offense to this. Instead we observe them surreptitiously; it is after all free entertainment, even if only of the lowest kind. If it seems that things might turn violent, we will cast spells without anyone noticing, weaving them with our fingers casually, or influencing them with our minds and the light from our eyes, in order to calm them and to keep things from getting out of hand. Otherwise, we don't interfere since it is not our business after all.

"The wind from a Dragon's flight stirs everything." Old Elfin Saying.

If during an evening out the conversation turns to books, movies, art, or even television or some other topic of opinion, we recommend those things that we like and that we think our guests may like as well. If they offer contrary opinions about something we liked and they didn't or vice versa, we don't argue. That's like arguing about why one person wears red and another green. It is merely a matter of taste and our interest isn't in insisting on people sharing our opinions and tastes but in understanding what their tastes are so we may give recommendations more to their liking in the future, as well as to get to know them better. We often find in listening to others opinions and recommendations that we learn much of things that we hadn't yet encountered and expand our knowledge and enjoyment thereby.

We elves tend to be vegetarian. However, if someone takes us out to eat and insists on us trying something that has meat in it, we will. The Law of Community is more important to us than our personal dietary restrictions and preferences. And if we take someone out to dinner and they wish to eat meat then that is their choice, we do not lecture them or refuse to buy their food if they eat meat even though we don't indulge ours'elves. Our devotion to vegetarianism is due to our own understanding of the laws of the Universe, and Karma, and the direction of evolution as spiritual beings. And if someone we know hasn't yet reached that place we don't try to force them to do so, anymore than we would try to force them to wear the fashions we happen to find pleasing.

If while we are out to dinner, we notice one of our party has food stuck between hir teeth, or on hir face, or has fallen to hir shirt or blouse or dress, or a slip is showing, or some other piece of clothing has become disarrayed that might cause embarrassment, we tend to draw the individual's attention very slyly indicating by gestures the potential problem. Alternatively, if gestures won't serve, we make an excuse to whisper in hir ear informing hir of the problem so sHe can deal with it with the greatest ease and least potential for embarrassment. This is especially the case if the individual involved is not an elf. For elves can be told nearly anything, and they will take it in their stride, even laugh, as they deal with it, but normal folk are very socially sensitive, having for the most part low self esteem. Thus particular caution must be used in dealing with such individuals. Our efforts are always directed toward saving people from embarrassment and protecting their, often fragile, sense of s'elf worth.

If we elves eat at an ethnic restaurant, which is actually quite common for us, and a server corrects our pronunciation of the name of a dish, we thank them politely. If they don't correct us, we will often ask them if we are pronouncing the words correctly, for we are ever eager to learn and expand our knowledge and understanding of all things. And it is also a great way to show interest in someone else's culture, which is nearly always appreciated by them.

If we are in the company of someone who begins to act in such ways that violate the social norm, we either enjoy the show, or become very quiet and inwardly withdraw from this person. If sHe becomes too obnoxious and inconsiderate of the feelings of others, we may quietly have a word with this individual. If necessary we will even apologize for them, since being in our company we have assumed a responsibility for this person, and we do what sHe should indeed be doing hir self. If hir behavior continues and sHe fails to heed our polite entreaties to act in a more civilized fashion, we will extricate ours'elves from hir presence as quickly and unobtrusively as possible and never involve ours'elves with hir again. We have known elves who would take the person aside and say, "Well, everybody has an asshole," or say to each other, "Looks like we will have to get the douche bag out for _____" indicating the individual by name. But these elves are too polite to say such things and settle for the direct approach, explaining clearly and simply why we'd appreciate a moderation of behavior, and framing it as a request and a personal favor to us, "We'd appreciate it if you would not do _____." In fact, we have seldom encountered such difficulties, but that may be because we don't often tend to associate with abhorrent folk.

Elfin Saying: The deeper you wander into Elfin the greater your luck becomes!

Chapter 5:
Work Related

First, it should be said that elves like to combine work and play. We do not separate our worlds as so many tend to do. We do not separate the material and spiritual worlds, nor are we of the opinion that work must be serious and play fun. We like to enjoy our work and tend to avoid things that we cannot find enjoyment and pleasure in doing, even if the enjoyment is only the pleasure of doing a job well. And our play can be quite serious. Our creative endeavors, especially, combine both work/effort and play/pleasure.

Second, elves are seldom found in traditional careers. You don't tend to find us climbing the corporate ladder to success, or being politicians, or bureaucrats. However, it does happen that as actors we may wait or bus tables, as writers we may work in some office or factory, as painters we may paint the insides and outsides of houses, and so forth. We sometimes have to do other things to bring in the money to keep us afloat until we can establish ours'elves in our chosen field of endeavor. The following guidelines of etiquette are directed primarily toward dealing with the various situations we may encounter in the work place or in dealing with work related issues and relationships.

If an elf receives a promotion for which a colleague was also in the running, we do not lord it over them. It would be rude to do so, and we try never to be rude. Rudeness in the elfin mind is weakness. Also, since we are just waiting for our big break in theatre, or our novel to be published, or to have a sell out showing off our paintings, or some other success with our creative endeavors, we don't really care. We probably got the promotion because of our mysterious insouciance in the first place. Our great fears do not revolve around getting a promotion and moving up the corporate ladder, but rather involve never making it on our own for our creative pursuits, and getting stuck in the system forever. We would have been just as happy if our colleague had gotten the promotion, or at least not have cared anymore than we did about getting it ours'elves. What is important to us always is keeping good relationship with everyone willing to be our friend, for we know that this is the true way to opportunity and success.

When a colleague gets a promotion that we were also in the running for, we congratulate them. Really, we are usually glad they got it instead of us. Of course, the extra money might have been helpful, but did we really want the extra responsibility? Usually, we elves are simply biding our time until we can work at what we really want to do. We, most often sacrifice money for the time to spend doing our own projects anyway. What do we care about promotion? It's getting that part we auditioned for that concerns us.

If a colleague has a problem with our getting a promotion, we simply treat hir with courtesy and respect as we've always done. We give hir time for this change to settle in hir heart and mind, and usually when sHe realizes our behavior towards hir has not changed, sHe will adapt to the new situation. If sHe continues to resent our elevation, and acts in secret to undermine us, that is hir own karma that will surely come back to hir in time. This does not mean we will not take action ours'elves in such a situation. If it becomes necessary, we will; but mostly we just let things be, and allow Time to work its magic on hir. Time doesn't really heal all wounds, but it does tend to make you forget, and distracts one quickly onto other things. Death and rebirth tends to heal most wounds, although some people hold on to their grudges, and thus karma, from one life to another. Greater fools they.

When we work at a place we always do our best. This is important to us, because we are developing a habit of excellence. We never undermine our co-workers, no matter how obnoxious they may be; we leave that to them. We never undermine our boss or supervisor. We maintain good relations with everyone. And when we finally succeed and leave, or simply move on to another job, we always leave with a hearty wave and a big smile.

Some people just like to talk incessantly. If we need to get on with our duties we can simply let them know we have work to do and that as much as we'd like to go on talking to them, we need to cut to the chase and get to the important data, question, or business aspect for which they called or came to speak to us in the first place. Saying, "Maybe we can continue this later," may also help.

If our boss instructs us to do something that is clearly not a good idea, or which we think will turn out badly, or for which we have a better idea, we will inform them of this. She may not listen and may order us to do it hir way, anyway, and, of course, if that is the case we will do so. And when it doesn't turn out well, we keep quiet. If sHe is intelligent, sHe will realize hir mistake, and correct it for the future. If she isn't intelligent, sHe will blame us for hir mistake, or blame someone else. SHe may even fire us, but then who wants to work for such a boss?

We elves never get involved in office politics. We simply don't care in the first place. It is all petty and meaningless, carried on by people who have yet to realize the wider nature of the Universe, and who have simply transported their Atlantean high school attitudes on into their adult life instead of maturing into a greater understanding of the world. Not to mention, they are probably bored out of their skulls doing meaningless crap all day long, and with that we can agree with them. However, they deal with their boredom through backstabbing and petty bickering, and we deal with ours by challenging ours'elves to find joy in what we do, doing it with excellence, and making friends with everyone who is willing to be our friend. This gives us the best chance for making friends and connections, thus finding opportunities beyond work, and also improves our chances of getting laid. Now, that's what we call magic. Besides when we become rich and famous they will all be able to say, I knew them when.

What An Elf Would Do

If a co-worker continually comes to chat to us in order to avoid doing hir work, we simply go on with our duties and only half listen to them, unless sHe is extremely entertaining. Most of the time these individuals simply want someone to nod occasionally, or say, "Um," while they babble on. They want to think you are listening to them, but don't really care if you say anything in return, in fact, would much prefer you don't interrupt their amazing discourse with insights of your own.

When a co-worker gets irritated with us for something sHe thinks we did wrong, or we did it in a way sHe would have done differently, we respond like a parent to a child having a temper tantrum, which is to say very gently, understanding that, more than likely, stress from some other part of hir life is creeping into hir work, and that hir complaints have very little to do with us anyway. Of course, it is true there are certain busybodies who always think everyone else should do things the way they think they should be done, and these we treat as though they offered an interesting opinion that we will consider in depth at our leisure. If we need to do so, we will inform them that while we find their suggestions interesting, we always make our own decisions and do what we think is best in every situation.

When asked to comment on the means to end war, the Great Elfin Sage Milovyn replied, "Make friends, create abundance and share love!"

85

When someone we work with has bad breath, or body odor it can be a ticklish matter informing the person, unless it is an elf, and then you can just tell them and they will thank you for doing so. However, when dealing with normal folk or someone with whom we don't have a close connection, we elves often look about for someone in the work place who can tell the person, and we speak to that individual and ask hir to quietly inform the person. The point is to save everyone from embarrassment, and the odor.

If someone in the workplace insists on sharing hir fanatical views about government, politics, religion, social philosophy, guns, or whatever, we generally listen very politely. We elves never engage in arguments about such things. We've probably mentioned previously in this book, but arguing with the fanatical, close-minded, and obsessed about their favorite diatribe is a hopeless, endless and useless affair. However, if they persist in pestering us about their pet peeves, theories or other nonsense to the point where we simply can't bear to hear it anymore, we often begin telling them about Elfland, elves, elven philosophy and so forth. This almost inevitably sends them running for the hills. These elves once had a family of skunks take up residence beneath our house. Alas, it was mating season and skunks when they orgasm give off the pungent aroma for which they are famous. We placed socks filled with mothballs soaked in ammonia at every opening to the area beneath our home. The skunks fled. Sometimes, you just have to give people a bit of their own medicine.

If a co-worker reveals to us sHe is on medication for depression, or going to therapy for mental or emotional difficulties, we think nothing of it. Almost everyone is on medication of some kind in this world, we're just glad the individual is getting some help. This can be a very crazy world and we elves don't judge people for going crazy in an insane world. In fact, it doesn't bother us if someone is s'elf medicating, as long as the medication they choose doesn't make them crazier than they already are.

If elves discover someone is surreptitiously tippling or getting high on the job, we tend to ignore it, even if it affects hir work. It's really none of our business unless by doing so the individual becomes a danger to others, in which case we have no choice but to privately inform whoever can take action about it to prevent greater tragedy. We elves hate informing on people, and would never do so except in such extreme cases where social duty compels us to do so. Some might think we should confront the person directly, but in our experience a person who would indulge to the point of endangering the lives and welfare of others is well beyond the point where sHe will, or is capable of, listening to reason.

If someone doesn't make an appointment, or call to let us know, we elves will, after giving them plenty of time to do so, contact the individual expressing our concern for them, and our hope that they are well and safe as we remind the individual of the appointment we had together, and our hope that the fact that they missed it was not due to any mishap, illness, or other unfortunate circumstance.

If asked to contribute for a gift for someone in the workplace, we always give if we are able to do so even if we don't know the person, for at our heart we are generous souls and we know that all we share will be returned to us multifold eventually. It may be that we cannot give much, and if someone should say, "That's all you're giving," we have no problem explaining, "Alas, that's all I can afford at the moment." If they have a problem with that, it is their problem and not ours. We elves cannot and will not be guilted into doing things we don't wish to do.

When asked to sign a card, or give toward a gift for someone who has been less than pleasant toward us, we elves sign or give if we can anyway. Although the person is probably too self-centered to appreciate it, we take every opportunity to smooth relationships between others and ours'elves. It's not that we wish to promote a relationship between us, but we do wish to move things to a place where we are under their radar and they heed us not at all.

If someone we know to be mean and ignoble asks us for a recommendation for a job that they are actually well suited for we will give hir a good recommendation, although we will only mention hir ability to do the job and not hir character. This puts the individual in a situation where sHe owes us, and also gives us a sporting chance of getting rid of hir, and never seeing hir again. Besides, the office to which sHe is applying may be filled with other repugnant folk, and sHe may fit right in.

When it happens that we elves are late for an appointment, we don't say anything about it unless the other person mentions it, although, for the most part, we tend to be on time. For us punctuality is an important part of the magic. When we give our word, we keep it. We are elves, and magicians/enchanters. Our word is our bond. If we say we will be someplace at a particular time, we do all we can to be there at that time. In this way our elementals will get in line for us. They know we can be counted on to fulfill our word, and we know that they can be counted on to back us up. Besides, it is not only bad business practice to be tardy, it is also rude, for it says we don't value another's time, and we elves never wish to be rude. If we have to be late, we call and inform the person if we are able to do so. If we cannot call, we make every effort to be there as quickly as possible. If we are central to the meeting, we will apologize for our delay, however if not and the meeting has proceeded without us, we merely slip in as unobtrusively as possible. If called upon to give an excuse for our lateness, we give a truthful but barebones account. They don't need to know every detail, but they do need to know that our delay was not due to a lack of concern, or appreciation for them, or the business at hand, but was due to factors beyond our control. There are, alas, magics more powerful than our own.

Often if a friend has made a mistake at work and we can cover for hir by taking the blame because we make fewer mistakes than sHe, or the boss likes us better, we will do so. This puts the friend in our debt, but that's not why we do it. We do it because we always seek to protect our friends.

ت

If someone is late for an appointment with us, we elves are very understanding. We know the world doesn't revolve exclusively around us, and we know that circumstances occur that often alter plans. Our main concern in such situations is really that the person is all right, and that the business we have together will be concluded successfully. All else is just minor details. If the person doesn't offer an explanation for hir tardiness, we don't request one. It doesn't really matter anyway. The important thing is that sHe has arrived and our concentration and focus now go to completing our business together in the most effective and efficient manner possible.

When a friend asks us to write a recommendation for hir for a job for which sHe is clearly not qualified, we always write hir a great recommendation, for it is our friend that we are recommending really, not her qualifications. She can always learn the job, or improve hir skills. And really it is up to her potential employers to decide if sHe is qualified or not. Our goal is to promote friendship, not do someone else's job for them. However, if we feel sHe may fail abysmally, we will ask hir if sHe really wants this job, and frankly ask hir what sHe will do if it should happen that the job doesn't work out. Again, our devotion is to our friend, not to the other company. Of course, it may be that in hiring hir and being disappointed the company may not take our recommendations with such great weight anymore, but what do we care, we're elves, this is only a temporary job anyway.

When we elves work for a company, we always keep its best interests in mind. We do the best job we can because we always strive for excellence in all we do, but also because we wish to help the company for which we work. They were good enough to hire us, and if we didn't think they were basically decent folk, or offered a decent product, we wouldn't be working for them. If they turn out to be less than fair to their employees, or fail to treat them with respect, it is their own fault that they lose their employees loyalty.

We elves generally have two times when we celebrate concerning work. The first is when we get a job. We always go out to eat on this occasion to celebrate our success. The second is when we leave, quit, are laid off, or fired from a job, which also to the elves is ever a cause of celebration. This puts things in proper perspective for us, for work in the world for others is always an adventure to us, part of our quest to find our way through an often hostile world on our way back to Elfin, were we are always welcome, and each and everyone's welfare and success is promoted.

Even if we elves lose a job, get laid off or fired, we don't leave yelling and screaming or cussing those who fired us. It is simply beneath our dignity to do so, and really our true job is our magic and creativity anyway. The worse thing we do on leaving a job is laugh because we know that without the grace of our presence a bad situation will get worse and their karma will soon descend upon them.

When we elves hear that a friend has left or been fired or laid off from a job, we always look at it as a sign that hir destiny points elsewhere. If we can afford it, we will take hir out to dinner to celebrate. If not, we will at least invite hir over to dinner to celebrate. While the loss of a job can make things financially difficult, it also gives us time to work on our own projects, art, writing, music and other creative endeavors, and that is a thing most wondrous. The important thing is not to be depressed about the loss, but to make the most of the time while we have it. It is sometimes hard, but ultimately we must have faith in our magic, our elementals, and our spirits and trust that we will be guided toward the situation where we really need to be.

≈

It is a very old tradition that whenever something goes wrong the person who was most recently fired, laid-off, or quit is responsible for the problem. This is in keeping with the ancient tradition of the scape, or escape goat, and who are we elves to tamper with such ancient and honored traditions?

≈

It is said that time flows differently in Faerie. That for those who come from the world and spend some time there, that years pass as though they were weeks. Which simply goes to prove the old adage that time flies when you're having fun.

92

If a colleague tries to solicit our support for a political candidate or cause that we are opposed to, we will often ask the individual why sHe supports this person or cause. Upon listening to hir answer we may ask another pointed question, Then another, Then another. We never argue. We simply help the person think about the politician, or cause, logically, which quite often is a difficult task for hir, and one sHe is not used to doing. Such individuals will soon realize that they haven't garnered our support, and will either leave us alone, or ask why we are opposed or uninterested. They will often try to argue with us, but again we will always respond with goodwill, and fair mindedness while presenting the facts, reasoning and logic for our position. If they can show superior reasoning, we may even alter our position, although often the facts we believe, and the ones they accept may be quite different, then the only thing we have left is the underlying good will of our relationship, and the fairness with which we've treated them. They may not agree with us, but they, if they are open-minded at all, will respect our differences. What we elves ultimately support is not a particular candidate, but the right for a free people to believe and support whomever they choose.

❧

People claim that we elfin are a product of someone's imagination. We don't deny this. We merely wish to point out that, that someone is Divine.

Sometimes in the work place we encounter people who tell ethnic, racial or religious jokes. If they are funny we will laugh. What we will not participate in is jokes made at the expense of others in the office who are sensitive to such things. On the other hand, we know that some of our ethnic friends enjoy a joke about their own cultures as well as we do. In fact, we often hear them from them. Still, we are ever aware that such things are often used to divide people, and that we cannot support. Did you hear about the elf who went into a bar and order a beer? No! Because most elves hate beer. How many elves does it take to screw in a light bulb? 100. One to screw it in and the 99 to help hir celebrate. Or. Elves don't screw in light bulbs, we screw in hot tubs. Not so funny? Neither are most racial jokes.

ॐ

If a co-worker asks us to lie for hir, it depends on the lie. Will it hurt anyone? Or does it simply save face for hir. Our ethics are circumstantially bound. Everything we do depends on the situation. We consider all the ramifications as best we can, and make a decision based on our best understanding of what is going on, and what the result will be relative to our actions. If for some reason, we can't or won't lie for hir, we simply tell hir we are unable to do so. This may make the person angry, but that is truly hir problem. If the person is really our friend, sHe will understand. If sHe is not our friend, then why is sHe asking us for this favor in the first place?

ॐ

The easiest way to get people to change is to accept them as they are.

If we need to speak to someone in private, we usually ask if we can do so. If others are around and we are in our office, we may politely inform them that we need to speak to the person alone. Among elves this is not a problem. We can say anything we wish in front of our elfkin, but we also understand in dealing with those who are not elven that some things are best revealed in private, and if we are not immediately privy to them, our elf friends will soon inform us. This is especially true if we need to chastise someone at work, or inform them that they are suffering from halitosis or something, we will always do that privately. Our intention is ever to protect the other's feelings, and sense of s'elf worth and dignity, and we never wish to do anything to embarrass them.

We elves are aware that certain individuals, often the police or other individuals in positions of power and authority, suffer from such low self-esteem that they always need to be called by their titles. Failing to do so not only aggravates them, but it also makes them cling even more fiercely to their title, which they use as a substitute for self validation. We always treat such individuals with the greatest of respect, not simply because they tend to be dangerous, malicious and vengeful if we don't, so great is their hidden and undisclosed feelings of inferiority; but because this is the only way to soothe their souls, and eventually give them a chance to give up such arbitrary and empty symbols of personal worth. We elves say if you wish a dog to let go of something, you don't tug on it.

We elves have a basic rule when it comes to names or titles. A person can either call us what we wish to be called, and we will call them what they wish. Or they can call us whatever they wish, and we will call them whatever we wish. Most folks choose the first option. Those that choose the second usually switch to the first. If someone asks us to use a title or honorific in addressing them, we will ask them to use our titles. If someone offers hir first name, we will offers ours. We ever seek equal and reciprocal relationships. If we are in a situation where we compelled to call someone by a title while sHe insists on using our first name, we will tolerate it, but don't like it, and we never offer these individuals our true elfin names anyway. For such individuals as these we use a world name, which is something we utilize while passing through the world, rather like a disguise. In such situations, and for such individuals, we are aware that we are really acting, that we are part of a play they have constructed in their minds. We remind ours'elves that we are merely fulfilling our role in their play, and that they don't really know us at all. It is not personal, and we don't take offense, for it is only a part we are playing, and we always do our best to perform our roles to perfection.

If you're not in touch with your own heart,
you can't really touch anyone else's.

Chapter 6:
Courting

S ometimes someone takes a shine to us although we find no mutual attraction on our part. We always try to be as kind and gentle as possible in refusing these individuals. In fact, if possible, we move the relationship toward friendship. We don't however say, "Let's be friends, " or "I think of you more as a friend," that makes friendship sound trite and to us friendship is never trite. Friendship is pivotal to all success and relationship, and the means to attaining nearly everything we desire. Nor do we say, "I just don't see you in that way," but we may say, "I don't feel that way about you now, but let's develop our friendship, and see where it leads to." Then, we keep them in mind when we think about our other friends and consider who among our friends might find hir interesting. There is always a bit of the matchmaker in the elven character. Finding our own true place in the Magic, means helping others find their true place as well.

≈

Among the Elfin

home and school are usually one.

As we've said, friendship is the basis of all elven relationships. We always strive for friendship, first and foremost. Some folks think that romance and friendship are antithetical, but elves tend to be of the opinion that romance is a waste without friendship. Romance for us is not just about sex, although sex is great and we love it. But friendship, which is love, makes the world go round. If we ask someone out and sHe turns us down, we don't continue to pester the person. We take no for an answer, but at the same time we always look to the future, saying something like, "Perhaps another time." Then we return the relationship to friendship, and unless the individual mentions going out to us, we assume sHe is not really interested. If sHe refused our offer to go out because sHe really had a prior engagement, sHe will let us know if sHe is actually interested. If hir excuse was simply a way of saying no without offending us, we appreciate that. Then clearly friendship is the way to proceed, for friendship, as we elves say, leads to the bedroom faster than chocolates and roses. If the person is offensive, and responds to our offer of a night out with something like, "In your dreams," then, one, we probably failed to establish a basic friendship in the first place, which in most cases we would have been wise to do, and in the second, we are probably lucky sHe said no. We are thus saved from spending an evening with some soulless individual with whom we have nothing in common, really. We never wish to appear desperate, and really, we never wish to be desperate. There is, after all, for the proficient elven shaman, wizard, enchanter, always the dreamtime. If we ask someone out and sHe replies, "In your dreams," we think, absolutely, it's a date.

಼

We elves are aware that much of what takes place in relationship, particularly in the dating dance, occurs subliminally. We are therefore keenly alert to such subliminal cues. We elves are enchanters who know how to speak to the unconscious aspects of the individual to soothe hir, intrigue hir, and draw hir toward us if that is our will.

We elves do our best to introduce our friends to our friends since we are of the opinion that friends should be friends, if you get what we mean. We have noticed that some folks, however, are always wanting to date beyond their type, that is big fat women are often in love with big chested buff men who don't have the slightest interest in them romantically and nerdy guys go for sexy, movie star girls with whom they don't have the slightest chance. If you show them someone who is similar in type to thems'elves but of a gender to which they are attracted, they inevitable reject these individuals and have no interest in them. Essentially, they are rejecting their own s'elves but this fact, even if you were to point it out to them, never seems to penetrate their consciousness. If they are open to our counsel, then we will give them hints on how they may transform thems'elves in order to appeal to such men and women, or something close to it. But often their unreal fantasies are accompanied by an unwillingness to change. They say they want to be, "Loved for who they are." We have no choice under such circumstances but to compassionately leave them to suffer.

Sometimes, particularly at public events, sloppy drunks approach us who proceed to hug us, and slobber on us. Again, we endeavor to be as kind as possible, while redirecting them elsewhere, and extricating ours'elves in a gentle fashion. We try to always deal with such individuals with compassion for beneath their drunken levity we know there is tremendous pain, loneliness and suffering.

❧

There are certain individuals that one cannot have as friends. They, alas, are simply too unevolved to accept into one's circle. We will keep them as acquaintances, if possible, but it would be a terrible mistake to grant them access to our intimate circle of friendship. We are always kind to them if we encounter them, but we never invite them out, or around, nor introduce them to our friends. They are simply not ready for such things and would only make a disaster of the situation if we were unwise enough to feel sorry for them.

❧

If someone forces hir intentions on us and continually pesters us for a date, we continue to politely refuse hir. The more sHe pesters us the clearer it becomes that this individual is not suited for us, and it is because of this understanding that we know that pestering others is a hopeless endeavor. Even if some should reluctantly yield to our attentions, it seldom turns out well in the end, and honestly requires way too much effort. We elves tend to like our relationships to be a bit more casual, and to develop naturally, requiring little but mutual attraction, and love of a good time.

❧

For elves marriage is not the big deal that it is for most cultures, unless someone is inviting us to a reception with free food and drink, and then we think very highly of weddings. For us, however, if the sex has been great for a good while, and the friendship has endured, we may move in together. If it happens that we have a child or two, we may consider getting married because it is often easier to deal with normal society when one has children if they are married. Otherwise, we probably wouldn't bother. We figure elves either wish to be together, or they don't. If they wish to be together, they will be, and if they don't, they'll go their separate ways. Children however, tend to change the nature of our commitments. We may separate as a couple, but we will always be united in our determination to further the needs, education and development of our child. From an elven point of view, if one party doesn't honor that relationship, if they use the child as a weapon against the other parent, or they act only out of their own greedy interests, and don't take the needs of the child into account, then they have lost their way. And if they had any aspects of elfin nature in them, it soon fades, driven away by their avarice and their lack of consideration for their others. This is a tragic thing, but what can one do?

Elves love romance. We love the courting rituals. We practice them all the time, just for the sheer pleasure of doing so. We derive pleasure from flirting in the same, or similar way, that many folks derive pleasure from "busting each other's balls". Courting is a game we like to play, and elves know that just because we flirt with each other, doesn't necessarily mean we're being serious. We're just having fun together. It is our way.

Chapter 7:
An Evening Out

We used to encounter these two women who looked very much alike although one was clearly older than the other. One time Zardoa (one of the authors of this book), asked them if they were mother and daughter. In fact, they were sisters that were born years apart. It would have been far wiser, he immediately realized to his chagrin, for him to have asked if they were sisters, thus if they were mother and daughter, it would have been taken as a compliment by the mother. A Lesson learned. While elves don't have a problem revealing our age, many other cultures do. It is usually a subject best avoided. Why would you need to know anyway? Either you like the person or not, what does their age matter?

৵

If someone asks us, do I look fat in this dress, outfit, suit, whatever, the answer is always no. SHe may look fat, but that is due to being overweight, not due to the outfit sHe is wearing. So no, the outfit doesn't make hir look fat, the fat makes hir look fat. But we are not about to tell hir this unless sHe confides that sHe is worried about hir weight. So again the correct answer is always, no.

৵

When a friend asks if sHe looks good in this dress, outfit, suit, etc. we always say, you look great, or you make everything you wear look great. But if we find the outfit unappealing we may add, but we don't think that dress is right for you, or goes with your hair, shoes, whatever. If sHe insists and says, "Well, I like it," then we say, "That's the important thing. As long as you feel good about it, it doesn't matter what anyone else thinks." We elves wear what pleases us. We expect others to do the same. Sometimes, it is true we will dress for our intimate others. After all, they're the ones that have to see it for the most part. But mostly we wear whatever we want. Though sometimes we don't wear what we want, if you know what we mean.

If someone compliments us on our attire, we always thank them. We love to be appreciated in every way: for our intelligence, knowledge, kindness, and even fashion sense. Sincere compliments are always accepted gracefully, as are insincere compliments. While the individual may not be totally sincere, or may have some ulterior motive for flattering us, we are always open to compliments, but never deceived by flattery. We accept the compliment knowing that in time the individual will come to learn that sHe was more accurate in hir praise than she realized.

If during an evening out, we elves notice that someone's bra strap is showing, we elves think, she's still wearing bras? However, if we think it may be embarrassing to her we will surreptitious alert her, or find someone close to her who can do so. If we notice a friend has his fly open, we casually get his attention without others noticing and motion as though zipping up our fly and nod toward our friend. Again, our motive is always to save our friends from potential embarrassment.

If we come across someone at an evening soiree who is wearing a toupee, hairpiece, or has a comb over for hir hair, we don't say anything. We tend to think comb overs are ridiculous, but we also know how much prejudice exists in society toward baldness and we don't blame anyone for doing whatever sHe can to improve hir looks. Thus, too, if we come across someone who is wearing a wig, or scarf, or has suddenly shaved hir head, we tend not to comment. This could be a fashion choice, in which it is none of our business, or sHe could be dealing with chemo or radiation, which is also none of our business unless sHe asks us for healing. At any rate, the rule still applies. We wear what we want, and expect everyone else to do the same. It all makes for a more interesting world. We elves are not now, nor ever will be part of the fashion police. We are always, if anything, the fashion outlaws.

Calm and patience achieve
what haste and hurry delay.

Elfin Saying

When we meet folks we've met before but can't remember their names, we have several options. One, we can say hello, but not use their names, hoping if the conversation continues someone else will mention it. This is seldom the case when it is a single individual, thus 2. We will remind the person of our name in case sHe has forgotten it, and usually the individual will respond by reminding us of hir name. However, if sHe remembers our name and we don't remember hers, we will 3. Politely ask hir to remind us of hir name. This third option is seldom needed because we often have difficult names to remember, and so option 2 is most often selected. The important thing is not whether we remember their names, or they ours, rather that we greet them like long lost friends that we've missed terribly, and are out of our minds with joy upon seeing again. We always wish our friends to know how much we value them, and that even if our memory of their name fails us from time to time, our memory of the times we've spent together never will. If the day comes that our minds fail our hearts will retain them, and even if we see them in another life, we will still instinctively recognize them, knowing we've never met them in that life before, but immediate know them as our very own.

❧

Some folks insist that we cannot be elves
because we are more than a foot tall.
We simply smile at them and say,
"We've grown".

We elves often have numerous names. We have names we use with other elves. Names we use in the world among the normal folk. If we are in a situation where someone calls us by a worldly name in an elven situation, we may inform hir of our other name if we think a relationship may develop. Otherwise, we just let it pass. If we are in a worldly situation, and someone calls us by an elf name and the normal person wonders about this, we simply explain that it is a nickname, or a name we use in role-playing games, or whatever we happen to think of that will pass for the truth, if the truth is something that they aren't as yet ready to handle or believe.

Most elves don't find ours'elves invited to formal dinners, but it can happen. We are mostly aware of the social customs demanded of those who attend such events, such as which folk to choose first, etc. Naturally, we find all such artificial social demands ridiculous, but that does not mean we will ignore them. If we find it important for business or social contact, or just out of courtesy because our host holds such things in great reverence, we will observe these niceties as best we may. In situations where we may be in doubt about what to do, we tend to follow the example of our host-ess, or someone who seems to know what sHe is doing that is close enough to observe. If we make a faux pas, we continue on as if nothing had happened. If they are so serious that they hold their rules in higher regard than they hold our friendship, we probably don't wish to continue knowing them anymore than they want to know us.

We elves tend to go to a lot of potlucks. Since one never knows what one will find there to eat, we always take something we ours'elves will enjoy, that way if everything else turns out to be totally unpalatable vegan or tofu dishes (not to say that all vegan or tofu dishes are unpalatable, but … .) we still have something to eat. And some times you find there is nothing to eat but an endless table of desserts. Of course, we bring plenty for everyone. We surely are not the only ones who like tasty dishes. Just saying.

When confronted with food that is inedible we elves don't spit it out, except when absolutely necessary, but either finish the bite or politely enfold it in our napkin. If there is a dog around that is sometimes a solution, however, sometimes even the dog will turn up its nose, in which case you know your decision not to eat it was a wise one. Unless the food is a danger to others' health, we don't mention the fact that we find it tasteless or unpalatable; however, if we are asked we may say that we had something earlier and we feel just a bit nauseous, but hope it will pass quickly (like in time for dessert or anything more appealing).

It is unlikely that an elf will find hirs'elf in a situation where, after dinner, the males and females are separated, the women to gossip and the men to have brandy and cigars. We elves don't like to be separated from each other, and we don't believe in arbitrary divisions based on race, religion, gender or even age. If we find ours'elves in such a situation the male elf usually gets a large brandy as soon as possible, and at the first opportunity makes an excuse to attend the gents room and then, with brandy in hand, sets out to find his elfin lady/ladies and share his brandy with her, if she is inclined.

Nor do we elves like to be separated from our children. We didn't have them so that nannies, governesses, or baby sitters could raise or look after them. When we go to social events, we usually take our child with us. It is true that they may not enjoy the same things we do, but that's what hand held video games are for.

And while we are on the subject, although this has nothing to do with eating out, we elves do not understand why normals raise their children until they are 18, and then push them out into the world. Nor do we understand why someone living with hir parents when sHe is in hir thirties is looked upon in a negative light. What's wrong with families living together? What's wrong with families being close? We don't get it. We look at the world where families have been torn apart and no longer even seem to care about or contact each other hardly at all, and we think, that's your superior world?

On the other hand, we quite understand that there are elves who were raised by normals or parents who are ever striving to be normal and who seek to ignore, forget, and not look at the fact that they are truly other. These elves, while loving their parents, simply need to get as far away from them, and their judgments, as possible so they are free to lead their own elven lives without criticism or interference. But, that is a choice. We don't care if children live with their parents or not. That should always be a free choice, we just find it sad that so many parents want to be rid of their children as soon as possible, and that those who do choose to stay with their families should be seen as losers and socially retarded for doing so.

When elves have special dietary needs due to allergies, or medical, or ethical considerations, we always endeavor to inform our host-ess prior to our visit so they will understand our situation. We let them know that we don't in anyway expect them to change what they are serving, we merely wish them to be informed so if we don't eat something offered it is not in anyway a reflection on the meal, or our appreciation of their hospitality. This prior notification serves to save everyone potential embarrassment. When we invite folks over to a dinner or soiree that we may hold, we always inquire when doing so if they have any dietary requirements or prohibitions, so we may plan the meal in accordance with their needs. They are after all our guests, and their needs are our upmost consideration. We know that there are some folks who expect one to eat whatever is offered to them, and not make any requests to alter the meal in any way, and will be offended if one does so; however, these are not elven hosts. We cater to our guests. We invite them because we love them, and offer our hospitality to increase their happiness. We do not invite them over to force upon them our own tastes and opinions about how things should be done.

If we are out to dinner and a friend asks to borrow money, or offers an opportunity to invest in something, we will only give them the money if we can afford to lose it. To us, lending money or investing is a form of gambling. The chances are we'll never see our money again, and so we don't gamble unless we can afford to lose it. It's that simple. If it should happen that we get the money back or the investment pays off, then that's wonderful. But we never count on it, nor do we hound the friend to get our money paid back, or rail at them if the investment fails. It was a gamble and we knew that from the get go.

If asked to make a speech or a toast at a social gathering, we elves usually can do this easily. We are great impromptu speakers. However, if one of us feels uncomfortable speaking in public, sHe can always ask another of us, more proficient in the art, to take hir place. However, if sHe is alone, or specifically asked to speak, and feels uneasy doing so, sHe should make hir speech or toast as simple and sincere as possible. If she speaks from hir heart, sHe is sure to say the right thing. And if sHe should flub it in some way, sHe need not be embarrassed, most will never remember it anyway, and those that do would be cads to ever mention it.

We elfin tend to approach the greater Spirits differently than most magicians. We do not attempt to compel the spirits to obey by the power of our will, as many traditional magi do. Nor do we, as the religionists, pray and bargain and supplicate with sacrifices. Rather, it is our way to charm the spirits with our elfin ways and thus enchanted they willingly bestow vast luck upon us.

Chapter 8:
When Drinking

Some elves drink alcohol, others don't. Those that do tend for the most part to prefer wine and liqueurs to beer, but that, too, is a matter of personal taste and there is no rule that says elves can't like beer. And you can be sure that among the vast variety of elves, there will be some who do. Our wizards and sorcerers often prefer hard liquor when they drink, but that's wizards for you.

If we come upon someone at a gathering who doesn't drink because they are an alcoholic, or have some religious or personal prohibition against it, we do what we can to find them non-alcoholic beverages. If they wish to appear to fit in, sparkling non-alcoholic ciders work very nicely; they look like wine but aren't.

If we elves desire to smoke while at a friend's, but we are not sure sHe would approve of herb, we retire outside to an automobile, or the nearest trees, or some other space where the pungent aroma of weed will drift away with the wind.

When we come upon someone who has been trying to quite drinking or smoking but feels tempted at a party, we encourage them to continue in hir resolution to quit. However, if sHe insists on drinking or smoking we will give it to hir, it is hir life after all, unless we know that by doing so an immediate problem of drunkenness or unacceptable behavior will occur. If sHe insists on drinking anyway, we will let hir know that it is hir decision, but if sHe gets of hand, sHe should know that it will be our decision to send hir home and perhaps never invite hir again. If driving home would be a problem, we will take away hir keys, or do whatever is necessary to keep hir from harming others or her self. Obviously, if things get to that extreme our relationship is over. We don't desert our friends because they have problems, however, if they fail to heed our advice about things so important to us, we simply cannot have them around.

If an elf doesn't drink or smoke and someone attempts to pressure us into doing so, we firmly decline. If the person doesn't heed our indication that we don't indulge, we ignore hir, usually by saying, "Excuse me," and leaving hir presence and finding our true friends to hang out with. If someone says, "What, you don't approve of drinking?" in a somewhat hostile way, an elf may reply, "I neither approve or disapprove of drinking. But I don't drink."

When elves go to a party where we really can't find anyone to relate to, but we don't feel like going home or leaving, we will often go talk to the trees. They are great listeners and always good to be around.

When we find we are at a party and become cornered by someone who not only wishes to talk our ears off, but also wishes to numb us with boredom while doing it, we elves are not dismayed. We find human beings fascinating, even when they are just babbling nonsense, but they are endlessly revealing their psyche and their selves in doing so. If we tire of this, however, we need only say that we're thinking of circulating for a while and do so. If the person follows us, we will just keep going from person to person or group to group until sHe finds someone else to put to sleep. Although, we also sometimes think this is how we lost the points on our ears. Normals talked them off.

While elves may get a bit tipsy, we try never to get drunk. This only leads to vomiting, dizziness, and headaches in the morning, none of which are our idea of a good time. Thus, we tend to drink in moderation and smoke herb instead. No vomiting, no dizziness, and no headache. However, there is sometimes a bit of paranoia. But what can you expect when you step into the astral planes where the normal rules of reality don't entirely apply.

Elves never drink and drive, or get high and drive, that's not only illegal, but rude and inconsiderate of other's safety. We elves never wish to be rude. Or only occasionally, and only in emergencies.

Have we mentioned if the police or some other authority confronts us, we are invariably polite, even if they aren't, although in our experience, they usually are. They tend to respond well to courtesy, after all, the need to be respected is part of the reason most of them became authority figures in the first place.

When receiving an RSVP, we reply as quickly as we are able. This is not so much about courtesy, as our ability to remember everything we need to do. If we reply in the positive, and it later develops that we cannot attend, we will also let our host-ess know as soon as possible. Now that is about courtesy.

❧

We elves for our part don't usually have RSVP events. It is nice if our guests let us know they are coming, but we always prepare plenty of food for everyone, and if we wind up with extra we use it for left overs, or more often send it home with those of our guests who'd best appreciate it.

❧

There is always room for more. If our guests bring friends, that is fine with us. The more the merrier. We elves don't do +1, we just do +. Although it is also true that for the most part we don't tend to have huge gatherings, usually we only get between 50 and 100 people attending our parties.

❧

If our friends tell us we have had too much to drink to drive, we listen to them. We call a taxi, get a ride with a friend, or find a spare bedroom or sofa. If a friend who attends one of our parties is too drunk to drive, we always have room for them to stay somewhere. There is always the living room floor, or some other nook to put them in. They're probably too drunk to notice anyway.

❧

When we are at a party or club and wish to ask someone to dance, we just do so, asking, "Would you like to dance?" Most of the time, elves don't ask people to dance. We dance alone, or we dance together in twos or threes or more. If others find our dancing interesting, they may join us, and are always welcome. If we ask someone to dance and sHe declines, we accept the refusal graciously. After all, there are many reasons a person may not wish to dance. She may not find us attractive, however, sHe could also feel less than confident about hir own ability. SHe may decline because sHe has had a bit too much to drink, or is feeling unwell, or is engaged in a committed relationship with someone. We don't judge. Whatever hir reason, hir "no" is good enough for us.

We elves don't cut in on other dancers. If they are elves we will simply begin dancing near them. If they are not elves, we leave them alone. If there is someone with whom we'd like to dance, we can ask if sHe is interested between dances. In the midst of a dance is not the time to do so.

If we are at the grocery store or some other place, and someone cuts in front of us, we usually just let it go. We could inform them that the line begins behind us, but most of the time we elves just think if they're really that desperate, let them go ahead. And most of the time, if we see someone come up behind us who only has a few items while we have a cart full, we tend to let them go ahead of us anyway. Of course, if we are in a hurry it is a different matter, but then elves are seldom in a hurry.

Chapter 9

A Few Words About Birthdays

*E*lves tend to give gifts on our birthdays. We are open to receiving gifts, but they are not necessary. However, we very much like to give gifts to those we love and cherish on our birthday.

If we elves receive a gift we don't really want, or have no use for, or is identical to something we already have, we accept the gift graciously knowing we can always return it later for something we do want, or save it as a gift for someone else who can use it. If it is a very personal item and it means a lot to the person that we keep it, we will naturally do so, for it is not the gift that counts but the relationship it represents. In those instances, it becomes an item of magic that links us together. And we elves are very aware of, and endeavor to be responsible concerning, all forms of magic.

Elves celebrate their birthdays one day for each year they have been alive. A 20-year-old elf gets to celebrate for 20 days, a 65-year-old elf celebrates for 65 days. You can see what a good idea this is and why we are, for the most part, inclined towards long lives.

When elves exchange gifts and we give, or receive, a gift of much greater value, we don't worry about it. Again, it is the relationship that is important to us, not the gift. The gift is only a symbol of the relationship. If someone gives us something that we really feel outshines our gift, we know that we will make up for it later in other gifts or favors we do for them.

∾

We elves, except when we are very young, don't always have parties for our birthdays. However, when we do throw a party every five years or so, it is usually a fairly big affair, beginning in the afternoon and going on into the wee hours of the morning. We call these our occasionally annual birthday parties. Of course, all elves are different. Some may never have a birthday party (not if we have anything to say about it), and some may have a party every year (hooray!). Some may have small parties, which is okay as long as we're invited, and others may have large parties, which is okay as long as there is enough cake and ice cream.

There are times when all we see before us is a vast and empty wasteland. And we could despair to see such longing and desperation. But instead we bend and plant the seeds of hope and possibility and love from which shimmering trees of Elfin shall grow.

Chapter 10:
Hosting

*U*nless elves are very rich, we tend to have potlucks for all events. However, even if we are poor and have a potluck we make sure there is enough of a tasty dish or two for everyone. This may sound expensive, but in such situations we get to keep all the leftovers.

Elves don't usually have timed parties. We tell people approximately when the party will start and approximately when we think it might end, but they can show up whenever they wish, stay as long as they like, or leave whenever they are ready. If they stay too long, however, they will wind up being part of the clean up crew, and if they come too early they will be a part of the preparation, but that is usually okay with most elves, and in fact many come early or stay late just for that purpose.

The Elfin read between the lines
but also beyond them.

We have never seen a heated argument at one of our soirees. After all, elves are not a bunch of rednecks. However, if we did encounter trouble brewing between two or more of our guests, we'd simply ask the main instigators if we could have a word in private and after having informed them of our desire for a harmonious atmosphere, direct them toward those whose company they may find more congenial. Again, we've never encountered this problem among elves. We tend to be a very laid back group, and while we may disagree about ideas, we are seldom of a sort to get into a fight about them, or even argue heatedly. Also, we elves consider it very rude to cause a disturbance at another's party. It just isn't done.

Shoes, or no shoes. Many folks have a place to take one's shoes off before one enters their home. Naturally, we elves take our shoes off if that is their custom. However, while we also have a place to take off one's shoes in our eald, we don't require others to do so if they feel more comfortable keeping them on. Almost always, however, people will take their shoes off anyway out of courtesy.

If we elves come upon someone famous in the street we don't tend to pester hir, or ask for hir autograph. That is beneath us. If such as these wish to introduce themselves to us, we would, of course, be open. But most celebrities, unless specifically out to give autographs, simply wish to be left alone to lead their lives without interference. We naturally respect that. It is the courteous, which is to say the elven, thing to do.

Generally, we elves don't smoke cigarettes and we tend to have homes free of cigarette smoke. It smells so awful to us, unlike certain herbs whose smell is fragrant and aromatic. Therefore, smokers are usually directed to a porch or lanai or balcony, or even out among the trees if possible. In the pouring rain or freezing weather, however, we might make an exception, or direct them to an open window. We are aware that tobacco is the grandchild of the spirit world and is used as an offering in many cultures. We even offer it ours'elves, sometimes. However, the tobacco we offer is natural and not filled with the poisonous additives that are in so many modern cigarettes. A person who smokes these is not only poisoning hir self, but also poisoning the spirit world. These individuals don't tend to stay near the elves for very long, or if they do they become inclined to give up their noxious habit. Faery lore says that elves are repelled by iron, but the truth is, it is cigarette smoking we usually find disgusting.

If one's elf mate creates a dish that turns out to be less than palatable, we often suggest that an almond butter and jam sandwich may be in order. Or we may say, "Hey, why don't we eat out tonight," a suggestion that is nearly always received with enthusiasm. If sHe feels badly about hir culinary failure, we reassure hir that if sHe didn't experiment, sHe would never come up with such great dishes sHe usually cooks. Besides, these elves are simple folk really. Many people might prefer fancy meals, but we elves love p and j's, spaghetti, and other simple foods that were our childhood favorites, and we will always be satisfied, even delighted to be served our favorite meal. And then there's also always pizza.

≈

123

When someone accidentally breaks something while visiting, we let hir know that our friendship is more important to us than a material object. Of course, we will miss the object, and if the individual offers to pay for it, or replace it, we will let hir do so if sHe can afford it. But really, the relationship is much more valuable to us.

☙

Even when we live in communities or communes, we elves don't tend to have house meetings. House meetings bore us. House meetings are the brainchild of anal retentives who want to control things by having everything organized. We talk to each other, one to another as we encounter each other through the day, and somehow things get worked out and decided without any need of meetings, other than casual encounters. Perhaps only elves can function this way. Not having meetings would probably drive normal folks as crazy as having meetings does us.

☙

We have a basic guideline in living together. If you think it should be done, do it. Don't demand that others do the cleaning if you think it should be cleaned. The exceptions to this, and there are always exceptions in Elven culture, is that if you made the mess, you are responsible for it. Don't expect others to clean up after you. On the other hand, we don't tend to have a schedule for chores and cleaning. If someone thinks the house should be cleaned, sHe starts to clean it. Other elves will surely join in if they are around. If sHe really feels sHe needs help, sHe can always ask.

☙

What An Elf Would Do

When elves have children, or teenagers, we don't demand that they clean their rooms, unless they choose to do so, which usually they don't. We do ask if they would mind if we cleaned their rooms occasionally, since we're the ones who would like for them to have a more organized room. And they are usually open to this as long as we don't do it while they are in the midst of some important creative project, video game, or other endeavor.

Speaking of children and manners, we elves don't order our children around. We reason with them. We don't hit them, nor threaten to hit them. We reason with them. We know there are those who think they can't control their children unless they beat them occasionally. We find this attitude both peculiar and, from an elven point of view, unattached to reality. We find that children raised with reason are reasonable children. If there is something they need to do that they don't want to do, such as getting a shot at the doctor or going to the dentist, we explain the reason why they need to do it. In our point of view, they cannot be effectively raised to live in a democracy if they've been raised under authoritarian conditions. Beside, to our minds, it is just polite to treat them this way. Also, we are well aware that they could have been our parents in a previous lifetime, or will be ours in a future lifetime, so we treat them as we would wish to be treated ours'elves, which is with intelligence and respect.

The quickest way to Elfin is being there.

We elves don't talk down to children. We treat them in a respectful fashion as intelligent human beings. It's not that we expect them to have the same knowledge or experience we have, or the same intellectual development, nor do we assume they are mature adults, but that doesn't mean they don't have the same intellectual capacity.

We elves consider it rude to have someone talk for length on a cell phone when we are out together or sharing a meal. So, we never do so unless it is a call we must take, and if so we always excuse ours'elves so we can speak without disturbing the flow of conversation among our friends. However, if an acquaintance does choose to talk with someone on the phone while in our company, we will simply continue with what we are doing. If sHe is so loud that it disturbs us, we may leave; but if we find the conversation interesting, we might just listen in. We love finding out more about people.

It is rude to use handheld devices while driving. This is the same as drinking and driving as far as elves are concerned, and those who talk holding the phone to their ear and driving with one hand. Or worse yet, and we've seen this as well, steer with their knee while texting or looking something up on the internet, are immediately added to our inconsiderate asshole list. This does not mean we will cease to be their friends, but before we ride with them again, we will have a sincere conversation about the advisability and wisdom of watching where one drives.

If we elves have a party and the neighbors come to the door, we invite them in unless they are totally loathsome, even then we might invite them in as long as they're not violent. If however, they merely wish us to turn the sound down, we will, of course, do so. It is the only polite way to behave. Of course, if they were decent neighbors we would have invited them in the first place.

Speaking of neighbors, we elves are not known as the Good Neighbors for nothing. If you are good to us, we will be better to you. It's that simple.

If our neighbors turn out to be less than nice to be near, we elves will cast small spells to help them find something they will like even better, elsewhere. If our neighbors move, we will cast spells to draw better neighbors to us, often doing so by placing a magic rock near the entrance to the house, or a magic rune/spirit paper hidden about the house, or writing a spirit's sigil on the door using spirit water, so it can't be seen except by those on the shamanic planes. As we say, Good Neighbors deserve good neighbors and we elves are always Good Neighbors.

If our neighbors get a bit loud, we usually don't care, unless it is in the very wee hours of the morning, and then if it only happens very occasionally, we still don't care. We are very much live and let live folk.

If young people are getting a bit loud in the street near us, we don't mind usually. However, if another neighbor begins yelling at them and threatening to call the police, we find that behavior usually much more obnoxious than the kids were being, and generally we regard it as an undignified way to behave. Yelling in public is not something that elves tend to do. Actually, we don't tend to yell in private either, although, sometimes shouts of orgasmic celebration may be heard emanating from our realms.

≈

Because there are some people who think that magic is evil, we elves are careful in what we reveal to our neighbors before getting to know them better. It is not so much that we fear what they might do or say, although in some extreme cases that could be a consideration, but that it might affect our relationship with them in a way that would not be beneficial to the relationship, or to their mental and emotional well being. Magic does frighten some people, although elfin magic does not frighten people as much as it once did. Thus we elves tend to listen more than talk when we first get to know people allowing them to reveal themselves as much as possible and seeking whatever common ground is possible between us.

≈

If a neighbor is playing music of a style or genre we don't really care for, we tend to listen to it anyway. You can learn a great deal about people through their music. And really, we elves like all music, although we do like some songs better than others. If we really tire of it, we can always turn on our own tunes.

≈

Speaking of being good neighbors, we elves leave seed for the birds, offerings for the spirits, and even a bit of dog food for the raccoons if they happened to come around. We are aware of not only being neighbors to humans, but to the flora and fauna, the spirits and elementals, as well.

It is possible, but unlikely that elves would hold a guest-only dinner with limited seating arrangement. If we did so, and one of our guests calls at the last minute and asks if they could bring another guest with them, we do our best to accommodate them, however, if there isn't room or enough food prepared we will let them know that unfortunately it isn't possible. We would suggest that calling earlier so we'd have more notice and time to prepare would produce better results in the future. And we'd let them know how very much we wish we could accommodate them, but alas, in this circumstance it just isn't possible. The same is true when elves arrive late at night hoping to crash in our living room or some other space. We will try to serve their needs if possible, but we have had it happen that one group showed up late when we already had a group crashing with us, and if there just isn't enough room, there just isn't. Again, we let them know that we wish we could be of service, and prior notice helps us to be so.

You can not be in touch with your own nature without being in touch with greater nature.

When having guests over for dinner, we elves don't necessarily separate our children from the adults, giving them their own table. Our children are allowed to eat where they like, which often means in front of the computer, video game, television or whatever they are currently passionate about. In fact, we ours'elves don't necessarily eat at a table, although we do so sometimes. But when we have large gatherings, everyone finds a place as best they can on a chair, or on the floor, or even a bed, or a table, if the tables aren't already being used to hold the food. Some even stand and eat. In fact, some may even dance and eat. They have certainly been known to sway to the music as they consume dinner.

If we prepare a meal and our children or anyone else wishes to eat something different, we do our best to fulfill their needs or wishes. We don't, like so many normal and other folk, insist that they eat what we have prepared whether they like it or not. In fact, with our children, we know what their tastes are and have already prepared something that is nutritious and to their taste. With a guest whose personal or religious or dietary needs require a different meal, we will also be glad to oblige if possible, however, they must understand that unless they have notified us in advance, they will have to make due with what we have on hand, or they can order a pizza. It doesn't bother us that someone doesn't like the food we've prepared, we don't always like it either.

If someone is rude enough to try one of our dishes and blurt out, "Oh, this is awful," or something like that, we will try the dish ours'elves and if it is awful, we will tell them we agree with them. If it tastes all right to us, we may say, "Oh, good, more for us," and then offer to fix them something else, which may be something quite simple, like a peanut butter and jelly sandwich, although for us that would be perfect. We don't point out that blurting out how bad the food is, is less than polite, some things you just have to let people learn on their own. However, if someone is consistently critical of our food, or other aspects of our hospitality, sHe would be unlikely to be invited again. In fact, it is unlikely sHe would wish to be invited. Really, it is unlikely such an individual would be our friend in the first place. Although, if such individuals want to bring something they think is better to eat, or to come over and cook and teach us how to prepare their favorite foods, we elves are always open to learning new things. Particularly, if they provide the food.

Elves generally consider it rude to cast magic on people in order to manipulate them to do what we want. We prefer enchantment, which is a form of persuasion, for influencing individuals. However, that does not mean we don't cast spells over the food and drink we serve. Although, these spells are of a general nature for love and happiness, health and success and really blessings offered with, or really in the food as a gift, just as the food itself is a gift of love to our guests.

Elves don't usually try to control the flow of conversation at our dinner events, and usually such events are too big, and the conversations too diverse, for anyone to do so. However, in a smaller more intimate setting, if we feel someone is dominating the conversation to the point of boring us, and the rest of our guests, we will subtly change the direction of the conversation, usually by asking a question, or a series of questions of another guest, or of the guests at large. Such as, have you seen ..., or have you read ..., or what do you think about ....? Some individuals will, none-the-less, attempt to steer the conversation back to the topics they love to expound upon, but we can be even more persistent in diverting them. While not all elves are extraverts and "talkers", we are nearly all proficient at channeling conversation as we will and if we need to do so.

It is always polite to introduce our friends to each other. Unlike some folks who have a set order for doing this, introducing the eldest first, we elves have no prescribed order for introductions. What is important is that those who wish to know each other are offered a link through us. Friends and connections are keys to opportunity and success, as all elves know, and once one has been introduced it is far easier to develop a relationship if there is a mutual attraction. Of course, elves are not beyond introducing ours'elves if need be when we meet a friend of a friend, or even introducing ours'elves to strangers if we should strike up a conversation. We also introduce ours'elves to waiters and waitresses we like in our favorite restaurants, clerks in shops we frequent, or anywhere else we happen upon someone who seems nice, or a bit elven or magical.

If we have two friends that we feel would make great friends to each other, we elves are joyous to serve as matchmakers. Of course, all we can really do is introduce them, after first having spoken of each to the other. Preparing the way is important in all things. But we cannot guarantee that the relationship will work out, that is up to them. We can but make the introductions, and do our best to encourage them to harmonize. If it should happen that it doesn't work out, then we will always encourage them to maintain a respectful and a courteous friendship, even if it is at a distance.

We elves know how to end a conversation. We also know that with many folks this is best done in stages and not as a sudden breaking off of conversation unless necessity demands it. The important thing is to cease to feed the conversation further, and to make small indications that obligations call one to other things. Some people will, of course, continue to talk to one despite this, but at some point, after several warnings it comes time to cut them off, and being prepared, they will accept this. Not to mention the fact that these folks are always eager to talk to one so unless one is directly rude to them, one need not fear they will be insulted. A simple, "We really must go now but we'll talk again later," should suffice, although occasionally one must start walking away while waving goodbye until the individual's voice fades into the background.

Some elves are extraverts and some introverts, just like any other group, but all of us know how to get a conversation started if we need to do so. However, often elves don't feel such a need. It is seldom that elves are compulsive talkers as so many folks are, and we are just as comfortable sitting in silence with people as we are talking to them. Silence doesn't make us uncomfortable the way it does with so many folks. Besides the world is never really silent. There is the wind, the birds, the sea, and the chatter and hum of life all about us. There is the whispering of the spirits, and all of it is to we elven like a symphony of life manifest. And it is true that we aren't always acquainted with sports, or the latest pop music star, or television personality or celebrity, but that doesn't bother us, we are not beyond letting people know that we don't know, for that is how we learn. On the other hand, we may not be able start conversations by saying, "How about them Raiders, or 49ers?" or whatever and have any idea what we are talking about. But we have found that people are infinitely interested in themselves, and we can always start a conversation by asking a question about them, even if they don't choose to answer questions about themselves, and some don't wish to do so. Some are very private folks, and many, under the influence of dark imaginings, are paranoid about giving out information to strangers, but at least we've gotten the conversation started. Even if they say, "That's personal," we can indicate our understanding and sympathy with their position and say, "I know, you never know these days do you?" with a simply smile. Either they will respond or they will withdraw and if they respond we continue, and if they withdraw we bid them well.

Chapter 11:

Home Among the Elves

S ometimes, in the world of stress, elves cannot help but be overwhelmed by the pressures of the modern world, and occasionally we get a bit snippy with each other, respond with a bit of irritation, or speak more harshly than we would have liked. When this happens, we try to apologize and clear the air as soon as possible. Of course, we are always endeavoring to develop our spirits to the point when we can live in the midst of the world and not suffer from its stress, but we are imperfect spirits, in process of becoming, and sometimes things temporarily become too much for us. The important thing is to get things back to a harmonious state as soon as possible. With elves this is usually a fairly easy thing to do. With other folks it is not always possible, for they will hold grudges against one forever. But then, that is why elves tend to live mostly with other elves whenever possible. Elves understand.

஧

Curious as it is, often the greatest barrier to
an individual entering Elfin is their refusal
to let go of their suffering.

Most elves are not really private folks, and yet we are. To each other our lives are open books, but to the normal folk who can be so paranoid, judgmental, prejudiced, and at times, a pain in the ass, we keep hidden those things that would tend to freak them out. Thus, while our homes are often decked out in elven and magical regalia, the outside of our homes can look quite normal if we feel it necessary, just as Faerie is hidden from those who are not ready to see it. Sometimes, our entrance way is also very normal looking or halfway normal looking, so if a stranger comes to the door they will look in and see nothing that may reveal our magical nature. It is up to each elf, however, and each elf family, vortex, group, to decide how much they are willing to take on as they encounter and confront the potential prejudices of their neighbors, or the Jehovah's Witless, or some other who might happen upon the fringes of their eald. At the same time, we have found that if someone does come into our eald and is uneasy about the magical trappings sHe finds there, we have no problem explaining that we love the Lord of the Rings, or we're into Role Playing Games, or SCA or whatever we think will soothe hir paranoia as we gently ease hir to the door and make a note to never let hir into our eald again. These explanations work for nearly everyone, for they are eager to accept the superficial seeming rather than confront the profound reality of our magic. And this is all true. We do love the Lord of the Rings, and while we don't all do Role Playing Games, or participate in the Society for Creative Anachronism, we think they're wonderful. And one can always claim to be preparing for a Renaissance Festival, that always goes over well and everyone is eager to believe that about us.

ॐ

If a telemarketer calls us we may or may not listen to them, depending on our mood. Sometimes, we listen while they waste their time. What we never do is buy anything they are attempting to sell. Occasionally, we will listen to them. We never buy what they offer, but we don't mind letting them practice their speel. Sometimes, however, we simply hang up. We don't say anything, we are not rude, unless you consider hanging up without saying anything rude, we just hang up. Sometimes we tell them to take us off their list and not call again. Sometimes we put the phone down and go on with what we are doing until they realize no one is there. This is a variant of letting them practice their speel, only we're not listening. We don't get angry with them, nor do we say something rude to them. They are, after all, just some poor person trying to make a living like nearly everyone else, and we have sympathy for that, but they are wasting their time trying to sell us things we don't want, and eventually they'll realize that in wasting our time they are wasting their own as well. Probably, just hanging up on them immediately is the kindest thing we can do; but we confess that we elves while always polite, are not always entirely kind. Some times, we may ask them if they have been saved and start ranting about Jesus, although there is a danger they may actually be born-again Christians and start ranting back. Religious enthusiasm, we've found, is also often a wonderful way to deal with the intrusion of unwanted authorities. They tend to leave quickly.

ॐ

The elfin say pushing the magic is
not nearly as effective as stroking it.

By the by, if someone comes up to us on the street while we are going about our business and asks if we've been saved, we often say, "Yes" and keep on walking. If they ask, "Have you accepted Jesus as your personal lord and savior," we may reply, "We love Jesus," and keep on walking. We don't say, "Piss off, " that is too crude, although we are sure it must be quite satisfying to those who do so.

෨

If Jehovah's Witless or some other group comes to the door to save our souls, we may listen to them for a while, out of compassion and courtesy; however, it is important to know that if you do so it is like feeding a stray dog, it will just keep coming back for more. At the same time, we elves don't have a problem listening to them sometimes and at other times telling them we are too busy to talk with them. And, really, they can be quite fascinating. They're often like people who have come in a time machine from the past into the future. They give us a glimpse of life 30, 40, even 50 years previous.

෨

If a friend calls during dinner, we usually ask if we can call hir back after dinner. If it is a very close loved one, we will often take the call since love and friendship are more important than food to elves.

෨

The heros of man are politicians, warriors, and sports figures; the heros of elves are artists, inventors, and great lovers.

We elves are multi-taskers. When friends come over, we will visit with them and continue to work on our creative projects. If they need something to do they are welcome to browse our books, DVD's, or bring their own creative projects over to work on. If they wish to talk while we work, that is alright as well, however, sometimes our work needs concentration, so they have to understand that we may ask them to shut up for a while as we focus on our project. If they wish to help about the house, they may do so, or if they just want to sit and watch us work, that is okay as well. After all, we elves love to watch people work. In fact, we love to watch people. We are great observers and students of human, and other, nature.

When people try to solicit information from the elves that we don't want to give them, we may tell them that we prefer to keep such information private; however, we are more inclined to give them an answer that is true but doesn't really answer their question at all. If they ask how old we are, we could tell them our age. Why not? But if we don't wish to do so, we may say, "As old as the moss in the forest," or "Older than stardust," or "Older than I was last time." If they ask how we voted, we may answer, "For the best candidate." If they say, "No, really, who did you vote for?" We repeat our reply. However, here's the thing. Such answers make the individual feel you don't wish to be close to them. So we only use these tricks with those we don't wish to get to know us better. And if it is someone, such as a business colleague with whom we will have a continuing relationship, sometimes telling them simply and sincerely that we never discuss politics or religion is the best thing to do.

If a friend comes over unexpectedly, we elves will nearly always invite hir in if we can. However, sHe must understand that if we are busy we will continue with our work. If she wishes to hang out while we do our work, that is fine, but sHe should not expect, and probably won't get the attention sHe would if we had known sHe was coming. Then again, elves love our friends and will sometimes drop everything just to be with them. Circumstances and need often dictate such situations. And sHe should not be surprised if we attempt to recruit her to help with this or that task.

When someone asks us how much money we make, or how we make our money, or other financial information that we may not be inclined to reveal, we elves don't say, "It's none of your damn business." We may say, "We really don't like to discuss our financial situation with others." But we are most likely to tell them, "Enough to get by but not as much as we'd like." Or, "We sometimes dream of winning the lotto." Or even, "Enough to offer you a cup of coffee." Or, "Well the Magic has been kind to us." Of whatever else might amuse us to say at that moment.

If someone won't take "no" for an answer, we will if possible say "maybe", or "We'll think on it," leaving hir with hope, but not certainty. This is a preferred response; however, in some serious instances we must make our rejection clear and unequivocal, with "sorry, but no," or "It just can't happen," or "Not possible," "Not interested," or "Alas, no." If this means they will no longer be our friends, so be it, and if it is a stranger, we are probably just trying to get away from them any way.

What An Elf Would Do

It is true that there are situations where an elf may have people in hir life that are obnoxious but one just can't seem to get away from them. These are usually called relatives, or in-laws, and what can you do but put up with them. In a way, that is what family is about. Fortunately, most of us don't have to put up with them except at family dinners around the holidays. If nothing else, it's usually an educational experience, and we elves are always eager to learn. And sometimes it is an amusement, and gives us something to laugh about for months, even years to come.

Sometimes, we elves have someone in our family or among our in-laws who, despite all our attempts to connect simply don't seem to like us, or who cannot help but judge us for being different. There is nothing to do but be as loving and kind as possible while leaving them to their selves. As sad as it is, if they don't want to know us, we probably don't really want to know them either.

There are certain extraverts who think everyone wants to listen to them. This often happens on planes, buses or some other place where we are, essentially, a captive audience. We elves are usually fairly tolerant in these instances, but if we really need sleep, or need to get something done, we will inform the person that, while it was nice talking to them (really listening to them), we have work that we just must get done. Or we nod our agreement as we close our eyes, put on headphones and drift off to sleep. If they wish to keep on talking that is up to them, but as far as listening, we're done.

141

Chapter 12:

Dealing with Transgender Individuals

*I*f someone of a gender other than one we may be attracted toward makes a flattering sexual comment about us, we are not insulted. We thank hir for the compliment and go on our way. If sHe persists in hir attempts to woo us, we may have to inform hir we don't swing that way, but that is seldom the case. Such individuals are more aware than almost anyone which way people swing, and they are only teasing us in the first place. We take it all in the spirit with which it is rendered, with a bit of humor.

When a gay guy gets snotty with us, we typically ignore it. We know that this is just their way, and honestly we find them rather amusing and loveable, which is probably why they keep acting like that since people often reinforce their behavior; but really, they are funny.

The first step into Elfin begins with desire,
the last ends with an embrace.

In the course of one's elfin life, an elf is likely to encounter numerous transgender persons, that is to say broadly speaking, individuals who have had a sex change, or are in the process of doing so, cross-dressers, and androgynous individuals. The question often arises, what pronoun we should use in reference to such individuals? The basic guideline is if the individual is dressed as a female, we refer to hir as she. The same is not always true of females dressed as males, unless they are clearly presenting thems'elves as male. When in doubt use neutral references. By this we don't mean using the pronoun It, but rather we suggest avoiding pronouns altogether. Don't call them sir, or Ma'am, or Mr. or Ms. or Mrs., or lady, or any other term that designates gender. If you encounter a group of transgender people, you may sometimes call them guys, as in, "How are you guys doing?" since even though it tends to signify males it has come to be used for females as well. If they object, simply say, "Beg your pardon," and use their preferred term. Elves are always endeavoring to help people become what they truly wish to be. If they are males and wish to be females, that's all right with us. Also, we elves see people as spirits more than material beings. We know that their current material body is merely a temporary manifestation or house for their soul, and it will pass. Most of us have been both male and female in various lifetimes, so elves understand, have sympathy for, and are at ease with those who happen to feel out of place in a particular gender form.

≈

Chapter 13:

Lesbians and Feminists

We elves love lesbians and feminists. Hell, often we are lesbians, and we're always feminists. But sometimes we find that some members of this group display prejudice against our male members. That is surely to be regretted. However, we've found that often the solution to this problem is simply to let them know we are elves. Once, in Berkeley, Ca. we went into a feminist occult bookstore and the woman running the shop stopped Zardoa at the door and said, "This is a woman's only bookstore. No men are allowed." He replied, "I'm not a man. I'm an elf," and she let him in. Often we hide the truth that we are elves because of prejudice in the world, but sometimes the revelation of the truth is the very thing that makes everything work out.

The Gypsy elves say: Be not like the wind that announces it's coming but like the breeze barely noticed as it passes by.

Also, these elves used to take weight training at a local Junior College. During some semesters the only weight training courses that worked with our schedule were the all-women ones taught by the women's soccer coach. Legally, men could not be bared from the class, but at the beginning of each semester the coach would approach each man and let him know that he would probably be happier in another class. All except Zardoa, whom she loved, and she always allowed him to stay in the class. It pays to be an elf. There is just something androgynous about most elves, so we often fit in places that men and women cannot.

Elves don't care to be separated from each other, and we tend to avoid participating in groups where only men are allowed, or only women allowed, or any other arbitrary grouping. Sometimes, we cannot help but participate in such groups if say, a friend or one of our children want to go and needs a companion. But for the most part, we avoid such groups like the plague. We don't even have elves only groups. An elves only group wouldn't be an elven group at all really. What about our brownies? What about our pixies? What about our gnome friends? What about the faeries? No, that just wouldn't do at all.

The Elven say:

The greatest musical instrument is the heart.

Chapter 14:

Rainbow Brothers and Sharing

Sometimes we encounter Rainbow Brothers. The Rainbow Brothers always want to trade for something you have for sale for something they've found in a dumpster somewhere, and that you don't have the slightest interest in. Beside which, it is usually nowhere near as valuable as what you have to trade, even if you were interested in trading. Sometimes we will do the trade just out of the kindness of our hearts, but mostly we just have to tell them no, it saves us a trip back to the dumpster. Not that elves have anything against dumpster diving. It is one of our favorite amusements. And we have found some great stuff in or around dumpsters. But being harassed to do unequal trades gets to be a pain, and if you make the trade it just encourages them to come back and try it again. Which is okay if the brother/sister is particularly amusing, but most of the time Rainbow Brothers are just a bother. We are not rude to them, of course. Our refusals are ever polite, even compassionate, but it does them no good to be encouraged on a path that, in the long run, is neither good for them or us.

೨

Sometimes we elves encounter someone who wants to share our space, use what we have, and if we tell them, "No," they'll blurt out angrily, "You just don't want to share," which means you don't want to let us use your space for whatever. Now, most often these folks haven't offered anything in return. They want you to share, but they have nothing, or offer nothing to share. Again, if it is at all possible and not too great an inconvenience we might acquiesce, just out of the kindness of our hearts, for we elves are indeed very sharing folk. But if we can't, we can't, and we have no qualms in telling them so. It makes them angry, of course, because like spoiled children they aren't getting their way, but that is a lesson for their souls. Therefore, when elves wish a favor from someone, we try to offer something in return. In fact, we try to give them something ahead of time, so they will feel inclined toward us. So, too, are we inclined to share if we can with all our others, for it is also possible in time we may need something from them. That is not our main consideration. Friendship and helping our friends is always the main thing, but it doesn't hurt to help when needed.

> After all, we elves always say the more we share, the more we have.

The Elven say: Love begins with friendship and resides there as well.

Chapter 15:

Dealing With the Unseelie

*T*he Unseelie Faerie folk have a different point of view about humanity than we Seelie Elves. They are often angry with humanity, and not without just cause, but they often also have accepted some of mankind's values, such as dominance, greed, and other aspects that make it difficult for us to be with them for long (although we would like to point out that being dark or unseelie is certainly not always evil). And in the long run living with them can be hell. As always, we try to be as polite and courteous as possible in dealing with such folk; but it always hurts our hearts a little to see those unseelie with so much potential as elfin folk who cannot let go of the negative habits they've picked up by being raised among the normal folk, or by violynts, the grede (greedy), and the grimlean.

If someone tells us we aren't elves, that we can't be elves, we may ask hir, "Are you an elf?" If sHe says, "No," then we ignore hir. If sHe isn't an elf, who is sHe to say who is or isn't an elf, or what elves believe or don't believe? We are elves, therefore we are the only ones with the right to say what an elf is or isn't.

These elves once lived with an Unseelie Faerie Woman. She had been raised by a violent orc and a gobbler (goblin) and just couldn't, despite all the love we poured into her, get over it. We once bought a washing machine together. All of us putting in money for the machine, but then she told us that if we used the machine we would have to pay her for using it. Even though we'd helped buy it in the first place. And we'd have to replace it if it happened to break, while we were using it. Can you imagine that? Rather than deal with the craziness of the situation, we did our wash by hand in the bathtub, stirring it with a long stick, and waited patiently until she decided to move out. What can you do with such people? And she was of the Faerie folk, but not, alas, an elf of Seelie nature. Boy, was that a lesson learned the hard way.

Elves consider it rude to insist someone is something other than they wish to be. If we encounter someone and we think they are an elf and sHe says sHe is a dwarf, then we accept that sHe is a dwarf. We may express an opinion, such as, "Wow, you seemed like an elf to me." But hir word is sacrosanct. If sHe insists sHe is a dwarf, then dwarf sHe is. Leprechauns are a bit harder to pin down. We have encountered leprechauns and said, "Ah, good to meet a leprechaun," or something like this, and they most often are very cagey about their nature. They almost never deny they are leprechauns, but they will almost never admit it either. Usually they say something like, "Well, people used to say I looked like a leprechaun," or something along these lines, which is as close as they tend to get to revealing thems'elves. Probably think we're after their gold.

Often you will find folk who love Faerie but cannot give up their prejudices concerning magic due to their fundamentalist background. Again, what can you do but treat them with love, nurture them as best one can, and keep the inner secrets hidden from them. Sometimes, we have lived with such individuals, but while they tolerate our magic, they are never entirely comfortable with it, which puts a bit of a kink in things. But then, that's not much different from dealing with the world in general for elfin folk. Most of humanity has put a big kink in the magic, and that is part of the reason we are here, to undo that binding, those kinks, those knots, so we can weave the magic as it could be woven into a tapestry of glorious Faerie. Again, what can you do with such as these? Well, the trick is to do most of one's magic without them actually seeing it. Rather like teenagers living with their conservative parents, only in this case it is as though the teenager is conservative and the parents are off with the faeries. Sometimes with such as these you just have to shine them on (an old elven expression).

It is considered rude by the elves to eat in front of others without offering them any food. If we asked and they don't, for whatever reason, wish anything to eat that is one thing, but to eat without even offering them food or drink is so far beyond the bounds of elven culture and courtesy that we elves find it astonishing that it ever happens, but we have had that very thing happen to us. Yet, we said nothing. We endured the rudeness and discourtesy without complaint. It would have been folly to do otherwise.

Often when one lives with those who love Faerie but are uneasy with magic, you discover that they want to take over the house. If they are renting a room in your place, they will soon want to move furniture into the living room and elsewhere. At the same time, they will begin giving you hints about how you should live, what the right way to be is, the socially approved modes of expression and interaction, what you should wear, and every other aspect of your life of which they don't approve. In other words, they have an irresistible need to take over the house, your life, and everything else. We endeavor to be polite, of course, but at some point you just have to tell them, "No." However, note that the moment you are gone for any length of time, they will rearrange the furniture, move their stuff into everywhere except your bedroom (usually they will respect that) and when you get back your whole world has been turned upside down. They are hoping, of course, that you will relent, find it too much to deal with, or really suddenly see the light and come to understand that Jesus is a home decorator, and thus it is meant to be this way. Alas, if you give in to this, it will be like giving in to Hitler. They will just want to do more. However, elves don't get angry about these things. We know how these folks are and we choose, often out of financial necessity, to live with them. And yes, we can't help but grow to love them, blemishes and all. But we also can't allow them to take over our lives, so we put things back the way we wanted them. We remove the things they placed about while we were away, like couches that we don't want in our living room. Note, we don't demand they do it. After all, it is we who want it gone, so following our rule that if you want it done you should do it yours'elf, we do it ours'elves. After all, they're usually too busy whining.

ॐ

Therefore, when elves live in a room in an already establish household, we don't try to rearrange everything. We don't try to expand out of our room, or out of the spaces designated for us. If we do have ideas how things might be improved, we suggest them to those who could make such changes, but we don't get upset if our ideas are rejected. It is just an idea after all and things were functioning, more or less, before we came, and will most likely continue to function after we're gone. Courtesy and persuasion are our greatest allies. Making friends is the key to all success. Trying to force things is never advised, and almost never prudent. Making demands is ignorant and inferior and we elves ever strive to be superior people, to be the best elves we can be in every situation.

It can be very disappointing for elves, as well as others who have spiritually awakened, who have realized their true elfin nature, to discover that those who awakened them are less than perfect. We all have our foibles, faults and eccentricities, and these elves have learned that though our mentors are not always perfect, we can still learn from them. The same is true of our other elven brothers and sisters treading the path along side of us. They will not always, perhaps seldom, be as powerful, magical, and perfected as they may present thems'elves, or think thems'elves to be, but they are still our kindred and can benefit from our compassion, sympathy and understanding. Remember, courtesy above all; it is a great and true elven magic. And though those who inspired you may not be perfect, don't let that tempt you to give up the path. If we avoid the faults we see in others, in our own behavior, we will be helping them on their path as well.

While nearly every group is proud to be what they are, we elves find it rude to go around announcing how special we are to everyone. We wouldn't tell people that we elves are the most evolved folk on this planet, even if we believed such a thing. Nor would we say our country is the best country in the world. Or, as we heard a witch proclaim in front of a large crowd one time at a pagan gathering, "Taurus is the best sign. It is!" All such foolish boasting is the province of teenagers in high school, and those who've never evolved beyond that period in their lives. Such impulses stem from Atlantean times, and that did not turn out entirely well either. Even if you think that you, or your group, are the best, it is rude to go around telling everyone about it. It is always better, to the elfin mind, to let others say, or think, we are the best. We are too busy striving to be our best to talk about it.

When people wear fake pointed ears these elves are not offended. Pointed ears are beautiful. Some elves have real pointed ears; however, most of us, because of a need to protect ours'elves and our nature from aggressively prejudiced cultures around us have had the points breed out through genetic selection, survival of the least pointed, so to speak. But theatrical ears are wonderful, particularly if they are done well, less so when they look corny. There may even be those who have their ears altered surgically to be pointedly elfin. If they can afford to do that, good for them. Or as the British say, good on them. We love pointed ears. We don't need to have them to be elves, but they are wonderful. And if we encounter someone wearing a fake pair well applied, we always compliment hir. Did we mention we love pointed ears?

By the same token, if we elves encounter someone who doesn't seem elven at all, but claims they are an elf, we have to accept them at their word. To us, saying one is elfin is always an aspiration. The individual may not have totally, or even hardly, obtained that lofty goal, as evidenced by hir behavior, but if sHe says sHe is an elf, we assume sHe means sHe wishes to be more elfin in hir life and character, and we do our best to encourage hir and set a good example for hir by our own behavior. It is not our place to say who is and who isn't an elf. Each individual must figure that out for hir own s'elf. However, it is possible, under some circumstances that we may point out that certain aspects of someone's behavior or beliefs seem contrary to our understanding of what we elves are like, but again only the individual can decide that for hirs'elf. And, if we do this we try to do it as gently, compassionately and non-judgmentally as possible. If the individual feels judged sHe will only cling to hir behavior, which sHe is likely to do anyway. It is only by giving such individuals acceptance for whom they are that they will feel comfortable enough to change. And there is always the fact that there are Seelie Elves and Unseelie Elves and while we are related, we are very different in culture, belief and our worldview.

If someone seeks to argue with us about what elves are, or what Elfland is like, we don't argue with hir. First, it is foolish to argue about things that are essentially a matter of opinion and personal experience. And second, Faerie is vast, ever changing and adapts its'elf to each one who comes to it. Arguing about Faerie is like arguing about the dream we had last night.

There are some folks who seem offended by those who wear faerie wings to festivals, or to high school, or whatever. These individuals proclaim that those who wear faery wings are not taking Faerie seriously enough. To us, these complaints sound like they are coming from some puritan old lady who is upset that you don't sit up straight in church. It is not that we don't take the magic seriously. There are certainly times for that. Like when we're doing magic. But, on the other hand, there is no harm in our minds that there are those who are also having fun with faerie culture. Those who wear faery wings are but children to minds, even when they occupy very old bodies, and should be accorded a certain liberal understanding and tolerance because of that. Besides, Faerie is filled with delight as well as awe and wonder.

If someone tells us we aren't elves. That sHe is an elf and we're not (which by the way has never happened to us, but theoretically) we would ignore hir. It is the right of each individual to say what sHe is, whether sHe is an elf or not, or whatever sHe may be. Even we don't usurp that right. It's just plain rude to do so. And no one has the right to say what someone else is or isn't, although we may have our opinions.

We elves consider ours'elves royalty. All of us. We are all royalty. We are all noble. It is not that we think others aren't noble, for the potential for nobility exists in all people. But we elves are particularly aware of our noble heritage. Yet, unless we are with other royals, and sometimes not even then, we never mention this fact. It would be rude to do so.

These elves are not offended by so called posers. There are those who believe that individuals who play elves in video games, LARP's, D & D, and other such pastimes without actually participating in the elven culture, or taking our culture seriously, are posers; and they proclaim they are offended by these posers and disparage them. But these elves are of the opinion that those who play at being elves, instead of Being Elves, living the Life Elfin, are just trying it out. They are like individuals who wander into Faerie, and wander out again. There is no harm in this to our minds. It is just youthful exploration. And it is rude to disparage them. Rather, we try to encourage them in their explorations so they will in time discover who they truly are, whether they be elf, or other. It is our job, as we see it, to guide them on their way (instead of being Unseelie pixies and leading them astray) and we always endeavor to do our best in all we do. The fact that they are pretending to be elves doesn't bother us. We are elves, and we still pretend to be elves sometimes, although that statement takes an elfin mind to understand. Besides, it is by pretending that we become. Pretending is doing. Doing is magic. And magic transforms us. We wave our magic wands and presto-chango, sparkling glitter and shimmering light, we are elves.

~

The Sylvan Elves say:

A tree without roots cannot live;
a tree without branches does not care to.

Elven kings and queens never mention their titles even among other elves and faerie folk. This is because elven kings and queens, especially, come to be so because they have dedicated their lives to our people. It is not a position of heredity among us, of blood or genetics; it is not an elected position in a strict sense. One becomes an elven king and queen when others recognize one's great works and proclaim one so. One can never say for ones'elf that sHe is an elf king or queen (except under exceptional conditions). It is considered rude to do so, and elven kings and queens, especially, are never rude.

Fantasy stories often write of a hatred between elves and dwarves or elves and grimlins, goblins and orcs. And while it is true that we are less inclined by Nature to socialize with some of these folk and while some of them seem to have an instinctive dislike for us; we never judge anyone on the basis of their race. We have lived with dwarves and gnomes. We have been friends with and helped at times by grimlins, goblins and orcs. We judge each person by the virtue of their individual nature and actions. That is the Elven Way.

Chapter 16:

Charity and Other Financial Issues

*A*s we've already stated, if a panhandler solicits us for money, we give if we can and if we have some change conveniently available. However, we feel no obligation to do so, except for our natural compassion, and the knowledge that we are One with the all of life and in giving to others we are indirectly fostering our own s'elves.

When we move into a new area, or wish to do so, we often give money to the homeless or street people. These individuals, interestingly, are often very attuned and close to the spirit of the place, the spiritus loci, and we give to them as an offering to the spirits of that area. We also often put a coin or two, or some other magic token or rock, at the specific place to which we wish to relocate. Additionally, we introduce ours'elves to the trees and other natural features of the area, including the statues of prominent individuals honored by the city, town or region. All of this is considered polite behavior by the elven.

If some charity or political party that we have already contributed to, requests a donation, we elves have no problem politely informing them that we have already given. If it is a charity or organization with which we don't feel in harmony, we also have no problem telling them we have already given. Not to them, of course, but we have given to some group surely.

When a friend tells us they have filed for bankruptcy, we are usually amused. We don't laugh of course, particularly if they are very serious about it. If they are worried, we will surely sympathize. But we have known faeries who went bankrupt and within months they were offered a dozen new credit cards, and established a new credit rating. Elves just don't see these things the way normal folk do. There is no disgrace in going bankrupt. Like the very rich we know it is merely another financial maneuver and is nothing about which to get excited, or depressed.

If someone asks us how much we paid for something and we don't wish to tell hir, we don't say, "It's none of your business." We may say, "We prefer not to talk about such matters," although this is unlikely as well. Probably, we will say, "Oh, we got it at the Good Will store," or, "We found it by a dumpster," which may actually be true. If it is clearly something that didn't come from either of these, we may say, "It was a gift from the spirits. When the gods give us a gift, we never ask how much they paid for it." Which is also true.

If someone gives us a gift, we elves always find a way to gift hir back. It may not happen immediately. But we don't forget the individual's kindness, and we will certainly reward it at some point.

ॐ

When we give gifts, we don't expect that someone will give us something back. We don't give to get, usually. But reciprocation is always noted and appreciated. However, often we are just fulfilling our position as distributors of recycled energy and items. If we find something, or are given something, which we can't use ours'elves, we always try to think of who can make good use of it, or needs it. We are always redistributing. We feel it is our duty to do so.

ॐ

When we elves have covens, vortexes, etc. we don't tend to have formal tithing. It is not that we are against tithing. When we eat out we are generous tippers. And we believe in contributing what we can when we can, and we expect our elven brothers and sisters will do the same. If we have a project that we need money for we know everyone will pitch in what they can.

ॐ

We'd love to say that we elfin are completely free of prejudice and hate but sometimes the most we can say is simply, "We're sorry".

If someone asks us to borrow something that we don't wish to lend to the individual, we explain that we don't lend this item out. When we do lend things and we need it back shortly, we tell them so. If we think the individual is forgetful, we will inform hir that we will remind hir when we need it returned. That way sHe will not feel embarrassed if we do so. If it is a tool and it happens to break through no fault of hir own when sHe is using it, we don't blame hir. Things break. We know that. If it requires special handling we will either demonstrate how it is handled, or volunteer to use it ours'elves on hir behalf. If the individual is inclined to misuse things, then sHe is unlikely to be our friend in the first place, and thus as unlikely to ask us to loan something to hir as we are to accede hir request. Untrustworthy folks don't tend to hang around with elves, usually. Our magic tends to arouse their innate paranoia. If someone does borrow something and never returns it and acts like sHe doesn't know what we are talking about when we mention it, it is not the loss of the item that concerns us so, but the loss of the friendship.

By the way, we elves consider it rude to bend back the pages or otherwise mar library books that we borrow. This is just plain rude. We wouldn't do that to a friend's book that we borrow and we expect our friends to be similarly as considerate with our books they borrow. So, too, we treat the library like a close friend. The library is a good friend. We love the library and we hate to see it, or its charges, abused.

Chapter 17:

Dealing With Death and Tragedy

We elves never say, "I'm sorry for your loss." Hearing someone say something so trite and common, like someone saying, "How are you doing?" but not really wanting to hear anything about how we are doing, just makes our hair stand on end and hurts our teeth. Honestly, if someone has suffered a loss of someone they love, it's probably best to just keep one's mouth shut and listen if sHe wishes to say something. If you feel it necessary to speak, a simple, "Sorry," is more than adequate and often too much. Saying, "I'm sorry for you loss," is the equivalent of saying, "I have no idea what to say, but this is what I've been told to say," which brings us back to, just keep your mouth shut. If you don't really know what to say in such a profoundly troubling time, don't say anything. If you have some business with them that you have to conduct then express your sorry for having to disturb them at such a difficult moment in their lives and get on with it.

৵

One never knows how a person may react to a death in the family. One elven sister when she was in high school was called to the principal's office one day with her best friend and informed that her grandmother had just died. Now, she'd known for a long time that her grandmother would shortly die so this was not unexpected news, and the principal informed her of this in such a serious and solemn fashion that she and her friend looked at each other and broke out laughing. Not at the news of the death, but the solemnity with which this news had been delivered. If we are not directly involved in the situation, that is to say, if the deceased isn't a person we knew, and are also personally mourning, it's really best to just keep our mouths shut and allow others to grieve in whatever way they do as best they may.

Elves for the most part prefer wakes. In certain tragic instances of sudden death, or the death of a child, we are stunned by what is happening, but in most cases where death comes as a natural ending of the life process prior to rebirth, we like to get together and celebrate the graduation, so to speak, of those we love. And quite often we see many of our kindred we haven't seen in ages at wakes and we like to get together, tell stories and jokes and in general enjoy ours'elves. In some circumstances, as we say, the loss is too profound to do more than sit in a kind of meditative daze letting our psyche absorb this painful change in life, and then often even words escape us. In such circumstances, when someone we know is experiencing such a loss the best we can do is offer them whatever assistance they may need and we are able to provide.

It is generally considered a bit rude by elves to try to pick up the spouse or significant other of the deceased at the funeral or wake/reception afterward. If the spouse makes the first move however, that is a different story. For some folks sexual release is a powerful tool for dealing with grief and a means to healing. Under such circumstances, a mercy fuck may well be in order.

If a friend's pet has died, we elves sympathize with hir grief. Animals are spirits, too, and also have souls from the elven point of view and they can surely be more loving and loyal than most human beings, so we quite understand the feeling of terrible loss at their passing.

When someone has committed suicide we don't tell hir loved ones, "Well, sHe'll just have to start over again." Or, "God, I wouldn't want to have to go through potty training again so soon." Both of which may be true, but is this the appropriate time to point it out? Instead, as nearly always in such situations, we tend to share the person's grief in silence and mind our own business. A brief and sincere, "Sorry," is best if we feel words are called for.

If some evil, arrogant, obnoxious bastard buys the big one, we try not to be too obvious in our joy, for they may have been loved or admired by someone else. Among our s'elves in private we may toast hir demise, but in public we find it wisest to be circumspect. Even Hitler had his devoted followers who mourned his passing, although in his case and others like him we may make an exception to this rule.

It would be a mistake, however, to think that we elves are callous to death or always take it lightly. We even mourn our plants when they die. We certainly mourn the trees and our forests when they are so callously butchered for profit. We definitely mourn the loss of species made extinct by over population of human society, industrialization, and the pollution of the oceans and the atmosphere. We mourn the loss of our culture from the millennia our peoples were compelled to learn languages other than our own, punished for speaking our own language, and compelled to adopt the religion and customs of conquering peoples, or being killed if we did not do so. We mourn these things daily and see the potential impending doom of all of humanity on the horizon, so sometimes the loss of an individual being that we didn't really know does not move us to pretend to greater sorrow than we actually feel.

የ

Unless one is suffering from an overwhelming sense of personal loss, elves feel it is impolite to get drunk at the wake. Drinking, yes, drunk, no. In fact, elves generally feel that getting drunk is a bad idea on almost all occasions. Not that we haven't ever done it, but when we have it has merely served to reaffirm our conviction that it was a mistake in the first place.

የ

Courtesy is an elfin magic that few understand but almost none can resist.

If we happen to see the ghost of the deceased when we are attending a funeral or wake, we don't mention it unless we are with those who would understand. We also don't attempt to speak to it unless it is our job to help guide it though the afterlife bardos. The spirit is usually on its own business and unless sHe wishes to speak to us, it is considered impolite by the elves to interrupt hir while sHe is in the final moments before sHe moves on from this particular life.

Elves often like to attend our own funerals and wakes. Of course, we don't have a gross material body anymore and most people can't see us, but we love to listen in on what people say about us, and particularly to comfort those we love who are genuinely grieved at our passing. We let them know that we will be looking out for them from the other side, and find them again as soon as possible when we are re-incarnated into physical form. This, to us, seems the polite thing to do.

It can be risky at times to dance in the world
and a smile is often suspect. But if we don't
take a chance with a skip and a prance,
our own hearts will always regret.

When dealing with someone in the process of dying, we elves keep our interactions with the individual short. After all, this individual is busy dying. If the person is in the hospital or at home and the process of dying will take weeks or months, we may try to visit hir, but we also accept the fact that sHe may not wish company. After all, sHe is busy dying. We do find however, that people who know they will die soon no longer have time for bullshit and do not require any of the usually social niceties that are common among those who are busy pretending they will never die. Elves often find the company of the dying comforting because we can talk directly to them and speak the truth and they will do the same for us. We find this quite refreshing. If they will let us, we will send them healing energy to ease their way. And if they request it, or sometimes if we just feel drawn to do it after they abandon their body, we will help guide them through the afterlife, or the between the worlds life, really, and on to a new and, if our magic works, more successful life to come.

The essence of Elfin is revealed at the end of every true faery tale. No matter what the challenges, obstacles, and dangers encountered on the way, in the end those who have been true to the principles of Faery always live "happily ever after".

Chapter 18:

When Things May
Turn Out Strange

When someone shows a photo of their child, grandchild or other creature that they adore who turns out to be less than socially attractive, we elves often don't notice. Elves tend to see people's spirit more than their bodies. We find all sorts of creatures beautiful. We even find goblins, and grimlens to be quite lovely at times. Pit bulls, and pug dogs and all sorts of bizarre life forms often draw our admiration for their looks, although not always their behavior. So when we are shown a baby picture, or the picture of a child, they are always cute to us, or actually fascinating. Human beings, dolphins, and monkeys, are all fascinating to us. Even Frankenstein's monster is pretty cool looking as far as we are concerned. So smiling over someone's beloved child, and surreptitiously placing a blessing upon it as we do so, is no problem for the elves.

The Magic always resents being forced but responds well to persuasion and charm.

If someone asks if the jewelry we are wearing is real, the potential replies are as vast as our imagination. First, it should be noted that to elves everything is real in its own way. Dreams are real. Fantasies are real. Fake art is real fake art. Synthetic clothes made of polyester are real clothes, although we tend, for the most part not to wear them (polyester or even sometimes clothes). Rhinestones are real rhinestones. So if someone asks, is it real? We are inclined to say, "Yes." If they are more specific and ask, "Are those real diamonds," however, the possibilities of replies increase exponentially. If they are, we might say, "Real enough." Or, "Don't really know." Or, "Haven't thought about it." Depending on how we feel about the person asking. If they aren't real, we may say, "Real zircon." Or, "Real fake diamonds." Or, "In some dimension." Or, "No, but I love it anyway." The important thing for elves is to be creative in our interaction with others, without being rude to them. Who knows, if they get to like us enough they might give us some real diamonds.

ॐ

It is often written that we elfin have no souls.
This is the most incredible gibberish. Not only
do we have souls but we are most often what
people refer to as "old souls". Perhaps this is
what confuses them. For we are so ancient
that our souls have attained a degree of
tranquility and quietude that it is
as if it were not there at all.

If a friend asks us if we think they are too fat, we don't say, "Yes," or, "No," unless they are clearly anorexic, in which case we definitely tell them, "No." It really doesn't matter if they are fat or not as far as we are concerned. If the individual is a friend, then we love hir for who she is as a person, not for hir appearance. Instead, we will ask, "Do you think you're too fat?" And if they say, "No." We may say, "Well, we're happy with you as you are as well." If they reply, "Yes," we may say, "Well, what would you like to do about it?" And offer whatever help or advice we think might be helpful to them. We elves are magicians. We grant people's wishes. We help their dreams come true. If our friend tells us hir dream is to be thinner, unless that is a danger to hir health and wellbeing, we will do whatever we can, and whatever is within our power to help hir fulfill hir dream. Elves are typically shown in movies and books to be rather svelte beings, and generally this is so, particularly for the Seelie Elves. But there is no rule, save good health, that says we elfin must be so. And among the Unseelie folk, who include dark elves, dark faeries, and even goblins and trolls and many other folk, there are many who may be more full bodied, as they say. What is important to us always is that the individual elf is doing what is good for hir, what is healthy for hir, and that sHe feels good about the way sHe looks. What others think hir is irrelevant to the elves, unless sHe greatly values their opinion.

If you want to keep your "head straight",
you need to keep your eyes on the goal".
Old Elven Saying.

If people tell the elves they are really a wolf, or a vampire, or from some galaxy far, far away, we accept that as a declaration of their inner spirit nature and inclination. We don't take it as literal physical fact, since they are standing there in a human body talking to us. But we do accept it as a spiritual truth, a shamanic truth, a psychological truth, just as we know ours'elves to be elves even though some of us don't have pointed ears, or conform to the various other racial features that writers often ascribe to us. We elves are basically a spiritual, rather than physical race, and thus we easily understand others from that same point of view. We know that folks that say they are vampires don't usually live for hundreds of years in their currently physical body, but if they continue on the path they are treading, they will in time and in other dimensions do so. They aspire, and as long as their aspiration brings no harm to themselves or others, we will gladly acknowledge it, and help them in whatever way we can to achieve their aspiration. It's what we elves do. If we feel someone is proceeding down what seems to us a destructive path, we will cast bindings to help steer hir another way. Although, often the only thing one can do is to withdraw and allow the individual to wander down those dark alleys to their inevitable dead end. As we elves say, there is both good and evil in the world. The proper place of good is to perfect its manifestation. The proper place for evil is to abide in non-existent potentiality waiting to be joined by those forms that perfection renders obsolete.

❧

We elfin think that the only true fool
is the one that doesn't admit it.

When an unwed friend reveals she is pregnant and is planning to keep the child, we congratulate her. What else is there to do? Elves don't put a lot of value on formal marriage and so a person's married status is of little concern to us unless we are thinking of asking hir out on a date. We do know that the more there are positive people in a child's life the better, so we will do whatever is in our power to help our friend to nurture hir child when it comes. We also know that children when they grow up tend to like to know who their parents are, so if the father isn't totally contemptible then we will, if our opinion is asked, always encourage the mother to let the father, if he wishes to do so, participate in the child's life. Yet, there is, to the elven mind, no one right way to raise children, and much of what makes the world interesting to us is its diversity. Besides, we always love pregnant women; they glow. We elves tend to love things that glow.

If a friend tells us sHe is getting married to someone of the same sex, we don't ask, "Why would anyone get married if they didn't have to for the sake of the children or financial reason," which we may well think. Nor do we say, "Hope you will have a reception and we're invited," although we're probably thinking that as well. In fact, if it is gay guys, you know they're going to have a great reception. We encourage all our gay friends to get married.

"There is no satisfaction without longing."
Ancient Elven Saying

We elves are very forgiving folk. If someone has done wrong by us, they need only sincerely apologize and do what they can to undo the harm they have caused. However, until they do that, we are not so forgiving. We are not inclined usually to just turn the other cheek. We may ignore them, for often that is the greatest punishment, and in most cases we just want the person out of our lives. But if they have truly done harm, we will call down their karma upon them, knowing full well that in doing so we are asking to be examined by the Lords of Karma our own s'elves, which is in part why we always strive to keep our own karmic slate as clean as possible.

We elves are not beyond revenge if we think it is deserved. However, we are inclined toward poetic justice and love tales where someone gets hir just due. Mindlessly striking back at someone doesn't suit our sense of aesthetic value. By the same token, if we have unintentionally done wrong by someone we immediately seek to repair the damage. We never intentionally seek to harm others for profit, greed, or even out of jealousy or envy. If we did so we would be lowered in our own estimation, as others are who act so, and we elves value ours'elves, our integrity, and our reputation very highly.

The only way to see one's faults
is to look at them.

Old Elven Saying

If someone, who we thought to be a friend, betrays our confidence, we know never to trust hir with vital information again. If sHe is particularly close to us and did this unintentionally, then we will speak with hir and make clear to hir in the future the things sHe should not relay to others. If it was deliberate, then we will never trust hir again, and we will gradually distance ours'elves from hir unless sHe shows a marked difference in hir behavior. We don't get angry, although we may, in a very dispassionate way, confront hir about it, and if sHe is truthful when we do so all will be well, but if sHe lies about it, our friendship will soon cease, although sHe may not realize this at first.

If a friend reveals to us that they are gay, we may feel like saying, "No, shit." But we realize this revelation may be filled with great import for them, so we are more inclined to say, "That's wonderful." If they ask how we feel about this we will tell them that as long as they are comfortable with their sexuality, we are as well. Elves don't really care what anyone's sexuality is, unless of course, we're trying to get into their pants.

If someone asks if we are gay, our response depends upon who is asking and whether we are gay or not. We may say, "Absolutely," or, "No, we're bi," or, "No, we're merry. The faeries are gay, we elves are merry." Or whatever might happen to amuse us to say at that moment.

Remember:

It is in darkness that the starlight is revealed.

If someone reveals to us that their child is gay and they seem uncertain how to feel about it, we elves often say, "Gay, that's wonderful. We're pretty happy ours'elves most of the time." Honestly, elves don't care what a person's sexual preference is. What we do care about is that people try to accept each other for who they truly are, thus we do all we can to promote tolerance, particularly among those who are related and should love each other no matter what, anyway.

We elves don't arrange to have quality time with our children or loved ones. To us that means that most of the time we ignore them and every once and awhile we decide to actually spend a little time with them. All our time spent with our loved ones, particularly our children, is precious to us and we put our hearts into every moment we spend together. To us every moment together is quality time. In fact, being together with those we love is our definition of quality time. Nearly everything else is just passing time.

People don't have to be elves to be friends of the elves. They don't have to share our opinions, our politics, or spiritual philosophy, ethnicity, nationality or race. They don't even have to believe we are elves or believe in elves at all; however, if they don't understand that we feel we are elves they are surely too out of touch to be our friends. They only have to treat us with respect as individuals and have the affection for us that we have for them.

Elven Proverb: Magic is as real as you make it.

If a friend is going though hell dealing with an ex concerning custody or visitation, we sympathize. We don't tend to say, "What a dirty bitch," or, "What a bastard," unless we actually know the dirty bitch or bastard, and know our friend feels the same way. However, even if the person is a dirty so and so, we always encourage our friend to be reasonable and polite in dealing with them. Often, this politeness does little good when dealing with a real abhorrent individual, because they are determined to be cruel, take revenge for imagined wrongs, and wreck havoc, even at the expensive of the child. In fact, they frequently use the child as a mean of doing this, and don't really care about the child at all except in the most cursory fashion, and then only to make themselves look good to others, and make it seem like them are good parents. Still, courtesy is always the best policy, even when dealing with pricks. It is true it most often confuses them, confounds them, and makes them paranoid because they can't understand it, and it is never what they expect or desire, but that, unfortunately, can't be helped. It shows that one is superior to them, which they hate; but that can't be helped either. It is not our fault, or our friend's fault that the other is that way, and we can only advise our friend to be the best parent sHe can be under the circumstances. Usually such behavior stems from unresolved, and perhaps unresolvable issues from the individual's childhood. All we can do is help our friend get though it, and ease hir aching heart as best we may, and to advise hir for the sake of hir child to always treat the other parent with respect, no matter how little sHe may deserve it.

❧

If someone we know is clearly off hir medication, we will tend to avoid hir until sHe is back on them. As much as we have sympathy for such people, when they are not taking their meds they become unreliable, unpredictable and we have no interest in hanging out with those we can't trust. And it does no good to encourage them to take their meds, since when they are off them they tend to be paranoid about whatever anyone says anyway. So we fade into the forest of the world until they have thems'elves back in order. If they confront us, however, we will tell them directly that if they wish to hang out with us they need to take their medication. Although, for the most part, elves tend to be a different sort of crazy than normal folk. Elves are often eccentric crazy. We seem crazy to the world, but really are saner than most folks are. Which those who are actually sane tend to realize after hanging out with us for a while. Normal folk, when they are crazy, are neurotic or psychotic and we elves tend to avoid such folks in our personal life. It is true that many elf and faerie folk are driven crazy by the world. This world can drive the sensitive fae insane, and we have great sympathy for these, but still there is little we can do except send them healing energy. And if they are so far out there that they would create difficulties for us, we just have to avoid them until they somehow come to their senses. Each elf must decide in such cases what hir own limits are in dealing with such beings, balancing the love we naturally feel for our kindred with how much of a pain in the ass they will be. Even if we do have to avoid them, we do this in the most polite, subtle and soothing way possible. We don't wish to incur their wrath, nor do we wish to damage them more than they already are, nor even hurt their feelings, but if they are not coming to us for therapy or healing, then it is not our business to deal with them and there is little we can actually do, save to avoid encouraging their negative aspects. Courtesy and gentle politeness combined with firmness is our chief means of dealing with those who wish to impose their company upon us.

ॐ

Elves don't, for the most part, hold interventions. We don't gang up on our others because we don't agree with how they are living their lives. If we think they are doing things that are harmful to thems'elves or others and they ask our opinion we will give it to them. If they do things that disrupt our lives we will make it clear that either that behavior ceases or our friendship ends. If it is one of our children... no wait, we raised our children ours'elves, so they wouldn't do anything to disrupt us. However, if they were following a path we thought destructive to thems'elves or others, we may let them know what we envision as the possible consequences of such behavior. However, if they are that far off track, then it is unlikely they would listen to us, and all we can do is magic, sending spirits and elements to guide them back to the true path. Ultimately, it is their lives, and their decision, and often it is more important to honor their right to make their own decisions, even if they choose things we think unwise, than to try to enforce our view of the world. We may be right about the suffering they will experience from taking the wrong path, and if we are, they will learn, in this life or another. They will also learn that they suffered not because they disobeyed us, or ignored our advice, but because they made the wrong decision.

ॐ

If someone comes to us to confirm a rumor, or some piece of gossip, it really depends on who the person is and what the gossip concerns. If it is one of our close elven friends, we will naturally tell them what we know of the situation, but we will also make clear what we know for a fact and what is unsubstantiated rumor. We elves love to hear gossip, but we don't tend to spread it. Gossip to us is like a scientific hypothesis, it is something to be researched and investigated to find out what the truth truly is. We elves are always more interested in truth than gossip, which is often only malicious rumors spread by the wicked to harm others, and we know this. Thus we are ever careful when receiving gossip and even more careful in passing it along. At the same time, gossip can be humorous and fun and sometimes a good indicator of where we should seek the truth. They say there is no smoke without fire, but we elves know a good fire produces very little smoke. However, when a fire is smothered it can produce a great deal. Gossip is like smoke, and when we hear it we seek the smothered fire that is its source. Quite often that source is a vicious and untrustworthy demon spreading rumors to create disharmony among us.

≈

The elves often like to play curious mind games. They love to be courteous and kind to those who are less than so and to watch while such people either relax and are soothed on their way or leave screaming and tearing their hair out in frustration.

180

When we elves receive what seems to be a backhanded compliment, we are careful not to react too quickly. Often, the individual didn't realize what sHe was saying and didn't mean it in a negative way at all. Some individuals, raised in normal culture think it funny and common practice to cap on their friends. This is a social practice we elves, for the most part, don't share. Most elves are actually masters at this game, and those who play it with us usually don't do so for long. However, sometimes we will briefly engage in such behavior as a lesson or warning to others. But we know that this behavior can quickly lead to hostility, particularly from those who suddenly realize they are so profoundly outmatched and are playing out of their league. So having shown them our power, we quickly revert to nurturing and reassuring behavior. On the other hand, if we perceive the individual did so purposely, we wonder if they wish to truly be our friend at all. We will in time distance ours'elves from someone who consistently pays us such underhanded compliments.

If we found someone has told a lie that can cause serious harm, we usually don't confront the individual hirs'elf. After all, sHe is a liar and is probably just going to lie about the situation. Rather we seek those who would be affected by the lie and let them know the truth and leave them to deal with it further, if that is their desire.

Wait not on inspiration, act upon it!

When someone lies to the elves, it is a most helpless situation for we are fairly in touch with the truth and it is difficult to deceive most elves. None-the-less, there are individuals who attempt to do so, usually to make thems'elves seem more important than they are, or cover up some foible or failing of theirs. Most often we don't say anything about this. We see their lies but don't confront them. If it is a serious lie, meant to harm us, or someone else, we will also note this and tend to distance ours'elves from the liar. We don't like sharing our time with those we cannot trust. If we know them in a business situation or some other circumstance where we will continually encounter them, we merely note that they are untrustworthy and filter all they say through this understanding. Again, unless circumstances demand it, we don't confront them, or even let on that we know they are liars. In that way, we deceive the deceiver.

We don't get angry if someone doesn't believe we are elves, and often in introducing ours'elves as elves, revealing our elfin nature to a new person, we will do so in a fashion that allows the individual to assume we are joking if sHe is more comfortable doing that. Or if the individual wishes to think we are into D&D or live role playing games, that's alright as well. However, those who in time proceed to be our friends soon come to understand that when we say we are elves, we mean We Are Elves. And even those who thought us crazy at first, or joking, or just putting them on, often come to realize that We Are Elves. Isn't it wonderful?

Elves don't lie to each other. We will, however, say anything we think will ease the way and make things work out well in the world, as long as no one is harmed by it who doesn't really deserve it. Although, we tend more toward deceit than outright lies, often using a person's misconceptions and prejudices against them, leaving them to conclude, usually erroneously, what they will. We don't lie to them, we merely don't bother to correct their misconceptions. You might say we allow them to deceive themselves, to think what they will, even if it is totally mistaken. To the elven mind, it is rude to tell the truth to those who would find it too disturbing, and even if we did so they would ignore it, or soon go back to thinking what they wished to think anyway. The truth is often like some phenomenal event that is so far out from normal experience that the individual soon forgets it ever happened. Encountering the elves can also be that way for many people. They soon rationalize their encounter with us stuffing it tightly into the pigeonhole of their minds even though we never quite fit. And what doesn't fit tends to disappear from their consciousness.

If we found someone has told a lie that can cause serious harm, we usually don't confront the individual hirs'elf. After all, sHe is a liar and is probably just going to lie about the situation. Rather we seek those who would be affected by the lie and let them know the truth and leave them to deal with it further, if that is their desire.

The entrance to Elfin is as open as our heart and as closed as our mind.

Most people cannot accept the idea that we are elves. They've been taught that elves don't exist, therefore, even though we are standing right in front of them telling them we are elves, they cannot accept this. Since we obviously exist, we just as obviously can't be elves, for elves don't exist according to the way they have defined the world. That's okay. We elves understand, and we don't try to force them into believing, for that would be a hopeless task. Instead, we allow them to accept us as elves in anyway that will work for them. If they wish to think we are crazy, we let them. How could we stop them? If they wish we are pretending to be elves, that's okay as well. We elves love to pretend to be elves, to play elves. It's one of our favorite pastimes.

It is generally confusing and disturbing if you awaken a sleepwalker. So one is ever counseled to lead them back to bed and allow them to awaken in their own time. It is for this reason as well that we do not attempt to disturb those elves who have as yet not awakened to their true natures. We simply sing softly as they sleep and know that in time they will come to realize that we are more than just a dream.

Chapter 19:

Dealing with the Normals

If someone angrily asks us, "You know what your problem is?" We elves often reply, "Why no. We've wondered for years. Please tell us." Although, the person seldom does so. In fact, such individuals usually go off in a huff. If they do respond, saying something to the effect of, "You're an asshole," we may reply, "Well, everyone has an asshole." But we don't add, "And you seem to be ours." Elves endeavor to be polite to everyone, even those who are clearly attempting to aggravate us. It is not only a superior way of behaving, in our opinion, it also tends to piss them off and frustrate them at the same time. They are perplexed because they don't get the reaction they expected, and don't know how to deal with it. They are frustrated because instead of lowering ours'elves to their level we treat them with respect no matter how little they currently deserve it, and that is something beyond their experience. If they have any sense at all they will yield to us. If not they tend to withdraw, angry because they were unable to manipulate us. But the simple fact is our responses are not controlled by their behavior. They may wander away mumbling incoherently to themselves, but that is not our responsibility.

☙

Some individuals are going to be puzzled by the elves. They may say something to us and when we don't respond as they thought we would, they none-the-less hear the response they were expecting and reply to that instead of what we truly said. In such cases, we often have to point out to them that what we said, and what they thought we said were actually two different things. This often takes several tries for they will be certain that we said what they heard in their minds and not what we did say, so repetition may be in order. This requires a certain amount of patience and energy, but it is often worth it to clear the air. Naturally, this process requires composure from the elves involved, for there is a tendency to feel angry or frustrated when dealing with those who are clearly less intelligent than we, as well as less in touch with reality. But developing composure is always a good thing, for composure is a great power, is associated with dignity, and will hold the elf in good stead in all occasions.

౷

There are those who complain that we elves contradict ourselves. But can the left hand contradict the right? The nature of life is paradoxical, so how can we speak the truth without speaking to all sides of a question?

Elves may encounter those who tend to project their own feelings and ideas upon us. This is similar to when an individual hears the response they thought they'd get instead of what we actually said, except that here the individual projects their own behavior upon the elf. The individual may, for instance, shout at the elf and accuse the elf of shouting, even though the elf is replying quite calmly and in moderated tones. Again, they don't hear the tone with which the elf replies, but rather they hear the tone with which they expected the elf to respond. More than likely, they are shadowing the interchange with past experiences and expecting the exchange to occur in the way it has always happened previously. But elves are not your average folk, and our responses tend to be surprising and unexpected for most folks. Again, this requires patience and composure as the elf calmly asks the person to listen to their own voice and the elf's voice to hear which one is actually shouting. And again, they don't usually get it at first. Normal folk can be quite slow, but then they have been terribly traumatized, and new and previously unexperienced responses are difficult f
or them to process at first.

We don't make offerings to the spirit world in order to obtain our desires. Our gifts are freely given because of our love of the spirits. If they for their part should return that love by granting our wishes, then we are truly thankful and consider ours'elves blest.

187

Chapter 20:

Among the Goblears, the Violents, and the Grimleans

We used to talk about the Goblins, Orcs, and Grimlens, always projecting them in a bad light, until a Orc sister going for a PhD informed us how racists we sounded and made the case that while some orcs, maybe even most orcs, might be as they are presented in the Lord of the Rings and other Fantasy stories, that not all were. And we realized that she was right and apologized profusely. We also realized that we were glad she was right for we also wish the orcs, goblins, grimlens and others to evolve to higher consciousness. To be and become the best orcs they can be in the most positive, creative, and loving ways. So from then on we didn't talk about certain magical races as being evil, but instead used terms to indicate certain behaviors that we encounter among people and which, at least temporarily, defines them as individuals. We speak of the Gobleers, or Goblers, who tend to consume constantly, and thus also tend to be fat; and the Greedies that are a sub-tribe of the Gobleers. We also call them Gobleers, because they have a propensity to leer at those for whom they lust. We speak of the Violents, or Violynts, because, well, go around abusing their spouses, and in general trying to intimate everyone in their lives. The Brutals are a sub-race of the Violents. And we speak of the Grimleans, who tend to be skinny little screw-faced fanatics who also go around proselytizing about their chosen religion, political party, or whatever. These folks are so crazy they will even kill other Grimleans if they disagree with them about religion or whatever. What is nice about talking behavioral traits is that no one has to be a Greedy. They can choose to be Other. Of course, some may make the case that they just can't help themselves and are not to blame for their behavior, and that may be so, but still their behavior should be noted and nearly every elf in the course of hir life will probably encounter one of these behavioral types. The following are some of the guidelines for politely dealing with such as these:

❧

First, elves don't tend to have pet peeves. We find peeves irritating and bothersome and prefer that they don't hang around with us. In fact, elves in general don't have pets at all. The cats, dogs and other familiars who associate with us are considered our friends and family. They are not our pets, although we may pet or caress them. But we also do that with our lovers and they're not our pets either.

❧

Elves almost never try to dominate other people or situations in order to manipulate things to get our way. It is not that we don't believe in the power of the will but rather that we have learned that will power is most effective when applied to ours'elves.

190

When peeves insist on hanging around us we often magically bind them and set them to some task or other. Peeves, in our experience, will never shut up if you don't set them to work, and peeves often love other peeves, attracting more and more peeves to them. Which is strange because peeves don't tend to get along with each other, but since they like to fight and complain the company of other peeves at which to rant is apparently some sort of social event in their culture. Peeves, by the way, are a tribe of Gobleers. Elves are naturally polite to peeves. Peeves hate it when people are courteous to them and often leave of their own accord if you are courteous on a consistent basis.

And when we say we are polite to people, we don't usually mean this in a snotty, superior and arrogant way. We mean we are genuinely courteous in a kind and compassionate fashion. Snotty, arrogant and superior normals and Unseelie Fae hate, but they also understand it. It plays into their struggle for self worth and recognition. But compassionate and gentle courtesy confuses them. They don't understand it and it finds a resonance in their hearts and they change or they give up and go away. Either works for us. Acting snotty and superior is not a superior way of acting. Only by treating the individual with respect as an equal can one truly rise above them. Think on this. It is one of those paradoxes of elven thought and culture.

"The new is often just the old in disguise."
Old Elfin Saying.

If you are involved with someone whom you can never satisfy, run. There are certain individuals that no matter what you do, what present you give, whatever you say, whatever you do except exactly what they want at each and every instance, it is the wrong thing. These are not elves. We elves call these individuals Bitches and Bastards. Bitches and Bastards are Hob-Gobleers, that is half Gobleer and half something else, often Violents, or Grimleans. You can never do anything right as far as they're concerned for their most basic mode of operation is to constantly find fault. Even if you do give them what they want, their satisfaction only lasts until the next thing they demand. And even if you give them everything they want every time, they still won't be satisfied because they despise weak people who give them everything they want. The best thing for an elf to do when involved with a person who is a member of the Bitch and Bastard tribes is to politely retreat. Don't take their calls. Don't give them what them want, and most of all don't get involved with them in the first place. If you are involved with them, it can be difficult to withdraw, because while you may retreat from them, they will tend to pursue you for a while. And they curiously find rejection attractive in a twisted sort of way. It is a dilemma, but then they love having you between a rock and a hard place. This is a ticklish matter for courtesy alone is not enough to deal with them. One must become very determined and firm with ones'elf while continuing to appear very pliable outwardly. One must firmly but politely reject any offers they make, and at the same time not fulfill any of their demands, all while appearing very polite. Eventually, they will come to think you are a weak and unattractive person and will find another's life to plague. In time the elf comes to recognize these types in advance and to avoid them completely.

Note that the members of the Bitch and Bastard tribes are vengeful and don't take rejection well, even while finding it perversely attractive. If you cease a friendship with a Bitch or a Bastard, they will surely tell you it is because you are inadequate in bed and always were, your penis or breasts are too small, and as well as any other thing they can think of to say to you in parting and will certainly tell their friends when they get a chance; although they probably have already and have been doing so all along. Don't take this to heart. And whatever you do, don't respond with heated accusations in return. They love/hate this and it just prolongs the relationship. Accept what they say politely without agreeing at all, merely indicating that you understanding what they are saying if you say anything at all, although, indeed, silence is often best. Certainly don't be hurt, or if you feel hurt, don't show it. Never give them the satisfaction, for believe us, their satisfaction is always fleeting and temporary. If you let them suck any of your energy at all, they will come back for more, and even if you let them suck you dry they will only kick your dead body as their way of saying thanks.

Alas, in extreme cases, members of the Bitch and Bastard tribes can be stalkers. In such cases unfortunately, the elf may have to move across town, out of state, across country, even change their identity to get away from these Maniacs. Maniacs are actually Hob-Grimleans, but are often closely related to those of the Bitch and Bastard tribes. And, of course, one must leave without giving them any notice. Here we have moved beyond polite, or Faerie society, into the world of the Violents. Forget polite. Save your life. We elves have been retreating from these Maniac Bastards for millennia.

By the way, the Stalkcurs as a tribe are related to the Grimleans and the Violents. Like all peoples they are varied. Some, perhaps most, are relatively harmless. They merely want to watch. Others are hob-Stalkcurs that are bred from Maniacs and these can be extremely dangerous. If you encounter them, courtesy is important, but courtesy is never enough. And, naturally, give them as little energy as possible. Let your courtesy be impartial. Never encourage them in any way. Don't be cruel but don't be kind either. Be transpersonal. You may have to contact the authorities, although that just lets the authorities know who to check out if you turn up dead. You should be prepared to defend yours'elf. Beside mutual love and interest, this is part of the reason elves, like other folks, hang out in groups for mutual support and protection.

The Peepers are related to the Stalkcurs, but for the most part, they just like to watch. However, unlike the Stalkcurs who like to follow people around in public. The Peepers always want to pry into the unseen. In a certain way they are destined to be research scientists, social scientists, even psychologists and psychiatists, perhaps even mystics. But for now they are just a pain in the ass. Since elves have no objection to public nudity, we also tend to be somewhat tolerant of Peepers as long as they don't actually come up to our windows. In our view, if we didn't want to be seen, we'd close the curtains. Although, Peepers have been known to install surveillance equipment in people's houses, bathrooms and other places and that gets to be too much. Big Brother, by the way, is a Peeper.

Drunkairs are a form of Gobleer. They are actually a spiritual discipline, if you can use discipline in terms of describing those that seek union with the Divine through nearly continual inebriation. As we've said previously we elves try to avoid them. They are not usually dangerous, unless operating a vehicle, and then they can be, and have been, deadly. We simply find their behavior a bit too sloppy for our tastes, but when we encounter them, or that is to say when they force themselves upon us, we endeavor to perform a firm but polite withdraw as soon as possible.

At this point we should mention the Stoners. These are also a spiritual discipline. Although again the word discipline may be not quite appropriate. But these are most often composed of elf-faerie folk; and unlike the Drunkairs, they are seldom obnoxious. Nor do they force thems'elves upon one. They mostly sit about and smile and don't bother anyone. And we elves tend to deal with them in a kindly and bemused fashion. Some of us even share their path from time to time. We are shamans, after all. However, the difference is we elves do tend to use discipline in our consumption of the sacraments.

Men, Gobleers, and others believe in Catcalls. They like to whistle, or shout out to those they find sexually appealing. When we elves are subjected to such behavior we appreciate their appreciation but it is not always wise to acknowledge it. We may in some circumstances do so with a polite nod, but even if we do, we keep on walking. Each elf must decide what is best and safe for hirs'elf in such situations.

Men, Gobleers, and some other spiritual races will also sometimes call out either in appreciation or derision of our elfin magical dress or raiment. If they show appreciation we will often acknowledge it with a nod or tip of our hat, if we are wearing one, but we still keep on walking. If they are derisive, we ignore them. We act as though we didn't hear them. We pretend their voices are like a ghost's too faint to hear or understand. And, of course, we keep on walking. If we happen to be stationary, we will ignore them until they insist we pay attention to them, and then we will listen but not respond. If they force themselves upon us in this way, the situation can turn dangerous. We withdraw politely if possible but there is always a chance they will follow. It is usually best to stay where there are other folk unless you have accidentally stumbled upon one of their lairs. Letting them speak in such cases with no response or neutral response is best. Clever elven quips are lost on these and never appreciated. The important thing here most often is not so much to save one's dignity but get out of the danger, although sometimes that means staying in it until a way out presents its'elf. S'elf composure and faith in the magic are vital in these situations, as well as an understanding of the subliminal cues and magical passes and the magical mind set that can neutralize the danger. Don't show fear, these folks are like dogs, they sense fear and go after it. Be strong, be flexible, be polite and be ready to make your exit swiftly but surely when it reveals itself.

&

"Every bird has its own song."
Old Elven Saying

Note that the normal folk are often prejudiced about our elfin raiment. This is also often true of those of our relatives who happen to be normal. They will tell us that really they are not prejudice, that they have nothing against the way we dress, it is the bias of everyone else around them they are worried about; but the truth is they judge us for being different because they are afraid of being judged for knowing us. Sometimes, if it is truly important to them, we will disguise ours'elves as normal folk, but we cannot help but understand that in wanting us to conform to the dress codes of normal folk that they are limiting their own intelligence, as well as conveying their own fears about not being normal. This is also often true of employers who have a particular dress code, not because they are prejudiced, they will tell us, but because they are afraid their customers are. Why normal society constantly caters to prejudice we are unsure, but it doesn't help it one bit when it is more important to employers how someone dresses than how they do their job.

The Elven Say:
"You do not have to be on top of the
mountain to know there is
something beyond it."

Remember, Gobleer, Grimlean, Violents, and many others can be very sensitive about their intelligence. They often feel extremely inferior about their intellectual capacity particularly around those who are more, or better, educated than they are, but they cannot acknowledge this. It is best not to demonstrate how intelligent we are for they resent it mightily, and often go to great lengths trying to demonstrate their own knowledge and intelligence. Some of them can be very intelligent mentally, but socially ignorant, or merely uneducated. Grimlean can be quite bright yet totally limited by their particular fanatical social or religious beliefs. They can be engineers or doctors and yet believe the most incredible gibberish concerning their gods and the nature of the universe. Courtesy in this case often means allowing them to pretend to be the smartest one in the room. It is rather like letting children show off to encourage them. It is best in these cases simply to appreciate them as much as possible in a very general and non-committal way. It is good to remember that while we are more intelligent than many folks, there are also those who are more brilliant than we, and we wouldn't appreciate them boasting about it.

≈

"You may think us cruel but when someone is rude to the elves we respond with courtesy and love which so baffles them that they are tortured endlessly, much to our delight."

What An Elf Would Do

You may notice that Gobleer, Grimlean, and others speak in various of their native tongues and terminologies at times, such as Gibberish, Gobbledygook, and other assorted languages, that we elves sometimes, but don't always understand, often concerning sports figures, automobiles or other exoteric aspects of their cultures for which they have a passion. Usually, we just nod as though we understand, for often while we are not fluent in such languages we know enough words to get by. They often do the same when we speak nerdish, fantasy, dreamtalk, or New Ageish. Although, they often roll their eyes when we do so, while we are generally too polite to roll our eyes, except as an aside to each other, when they engage in various forms of Jargonese. Elves therefore consider it courteous to use common speech, understandable by all when in mixed company.

There are also the Bullies, who are related to the Gobleer and the Violents. They are, of course, best avoided, but occasionally one runs into them anyway and must stand up to them. This is especially true for our young who often encounter them in schools, which is part of the reason we elves often homeschool. Alas, they will only pick on those they know they can beat up. However, if one fights back, even if the elf loses they will usually leave hir along in the future. Bullies are essentially cowards and they don't like getting hurt even if they win. In the adult world one may also need to stand up to them if one is unable to retreat. One's willingness to fight usually deters them. However, remember they nearly always begin with words and insults, testing one. If one remains neutral and composed while speaking courteously, the potential conflict can usually be avoided.

ঌ

Certainly, every elf has encountered a Grump or two in hir life. Probably more, since Grumps curiously are quite prolific. It's hard to imagine anyone having sex with them, but apparently it happens. Grumps are related to the Grimlean but seldom so fanatical. They are merely unhappy about everything, are always Grumpy, where do you think that term comes from, and ever complaining. While you are unlikely to change a Grump's disposition, courtesy does help one deal with them. They respond well to courtesy, which is to say they continue to complain and grumble, but it does have subtle effects on them, and they are often curiously disposed toward the elves because of our dignified and polite behavior as long as they haven't been off their medication for too long. The Grumbles, by the way, are a related tribe and pretty much the same as the Grumps, and it is hard to tell them apart except that the Grumbles have a tendency to muttering. The Gripes are so similar to the Grumbles and the Grumps that only they can tell thems'elves apart. It may sound prejudice but to the elves they all seem very much alike. Also, you may have encountered the Grouches, who are another tribe of these folks.

ॐ

It is only fair that we give them due credit. For we must admit that the gremlins and goblins seem to have a natural talent for bureaucracy.

Curmudgeon is the Gobleer and Grimlean word for wizard. Gobleer and Grimlean wizards can be quite brilliant but they are also incredibly irascible. Somehow, they think of thems'elves as lovable eccentrics, and while elves tend to honor their brilliance and eccentricities, we still think they are irritating. In a way they are like one of those ugly dogs for which one can't help but have a bit of affection. Courtesy is good with such as these, but they consider it their due. However, while they feel it is their right to be offensive to everyone regardless of race, creed or nation of origin, and their right to make offensive remarks about everyone, they are incredibly sensitive and take offence easily. Be careful around them for they can be very vengeful if crossed. As we say, courtesy helps, but they are particularly prone to appreciation for their knowledge and brilliance. You don't need to fake it, in fact, we advise you not to insincerely flatter them. But a genuine appreciation of their very real abilities, nearly always goes over well with them, although it is quite possible the only recognition you will receive concerning this in return is a grunt.

The Doomers are related to the Grimlean and like to stand on the sidewalk with signs, or sometimes ranting, that the world is soon coming to an end. Isn't it always? If you wish to waste your time you could stand and listen to them, or even try to discuss the apocalypse with them, its pros and cons, etc. but mostly it is best to just keep moving. Fortunately, they don't tend to follow one, and if they do so it is only for a few feet. It is all right to smile or wave at them if you wish, but it won't make any difference and doesn't matter since the end is nigh anyway.

The Glooms are related to the Doomers, but have a more generalize sense of doom about them. They don't necessarily believe the world will end soon, although that wouldn't surprise them, except for the fact that life sucks, it's always sucked in their opinion, and it always will. Thus they believe the world is unlikely to end soon because that would just be too easy. There is a natural attraction between the Doomers and the Glooms, as one might imagine, despite their differences, and their tendency to think that life isn't worth living so why get together anyway. When they breed they tend to produce Doomangloomers who know that life sucks, will end soon, and then we'll all go to hell. No, wait. This is hell. Being around them certainly tends to be hell for the elven. What can you do but shake it off and move on.

Snarls, Sneers and Scowlers are all related to each other, and to the Violents and the Bullies, but they tend to be too small usually to bully anyone and have taken to looking scornfully at them instead. Actually, they tend to have somewhat greater intelligence than most Violents and Bullies, who can have native intelligence but it becomes repressed by their low social intelligence. The Snarls, Sneers and Scowlers love to function in bureaucracies. They become Hall Monitors in High School and eventually Vice-Principals. A lot of them like to work at the DMV. The position of movie or theatre critic seems to appeal to them if they can snag that job. Once again, being polite goes a long way to easing one's dealings with them, although one should not expect more than a suspicious and scornful look in response.

We elves have a certain compassion for the Touchy-Feelees, particularly if they are old. They will tend to paw one, surreptitiously find some reason to overly hug us, or touch us in some way. If they don't go to far we simply tolerate them. As we say, we feel sorry for them. They are desperate for connection and we understand. On the other hand, it just doesn't do to let them get you or find you on your own, or to let them corner you. Polite firmness is often called for when dealing with these. Retreat is often necessary. Sometimes you just have to take their hand and remove it. Each elf has to decide how far hir compassion will go in relation to Touchy-Feelees.

The Molesttears are hard to spot. They hide well and there is nothing to do if you encounter one except keep a close eye on them and your children and call the authorities if they approach. They are often related to the Gobleers. Similar to them are the Grimcestors who are related to the Grims. Statistically, most adult child incest takes place among fundamentalist families. We knew a fellow of Muslim religion who when the subject of child molest came up told us that where he came from it was so common that it wasn't even worth talking about, that nearly everyone got molested and you just needed to get over it. We swear he told us this. We are duly appalled. Now, elves don't care what happens between consenting adults. If siblings, or cousins, or whatever want to go at it, what do we care, although procreation in those circumstances is usually ill advised. But we are always opposed to non-consenting relationships. Be careful around the Grimlean. Keep a watchful eye on the children.

The Highway Trolls, on the other hand, respond well to courtesy. In fact, they demand it and will get very out of sorts if they think you are treating them with disrespect. At the same time, a polite, friendly and cooperative response goes down well with them and sometimes even touches their hearts, and they will let much slide for those who are courteous to them.

అ

And while elves feel Troll booths, most often located on bridges as is traditional with trolls, are organized highway robbery, it's no use complaining. Simply pay the troll the fee to pass and go on. It is true that in Elfin the ways are always Free Ways. But often we must pass though the world and have no choice but to pay their tolls. And again, simple courtesy, while it makes no difference, is always advised. You have to pay the toll whether you like it or not, whether you're grumpy or happy, so why not do it politely. If you try to evade the toll they will send the Highway Pay Trolls after you and no amount of courtesy will help you from their wrath if you haven't paid up.

అ

And you may wish to note that in the Grimlean, Gobleer, Violent, and other languages the words for Elf and Faerie are weirdo, queer, faggot, crazy, hippie, freak (which is also a word we use for ours'elves) and yes, fairy. So if someone calls you one of these words know that 1. They are speaking in Grimlean or Gobleer, etc. and 2. They have actually recognized you are of elf or faerie kind. You may feel insulted but mostly we ignore them and pretend we don't understand their language, which for the most part is true. Who, but they, can understand Prejudis and Discrimatese (some of the common languages of Grimlean, Gobleers and Violents)?

If elves forget an anniversary or a birthday, it's no big deal if they are involved with another elf. Elves will happily remind each other of our anniversaries in case someone has forgotten, and we will often tell people of an impending birthday weeks before it occurs, just so they'll remember and not be embarrassed that they forgot. See how thoughtful we are? However, if you are involved with a normal, or some other spiritual race, it is important to note that the forgetting of birthdays and anniversaries is close to treason and they will make you suffer for it. They will put you in the doghouse. Which, we think is nice that they have houses for their dogs, although we tend to let our dogs live with us and don't want to be separate from them. Although, apparently their doghouses are usually very small so it is hard to fit in them, and it can be quite cold in the wintertime. So, if you are in a relationship with a normal or other, don't forget the anniversary. They will expect you to do a lot of polite groveling to make up for it if you do forget, but even that won't be enough. And they will torture you for days, even weeks, about it. In fact, some of them will carry this around for years, bringing it up whenever they wish to torture you a bit more. Or they will mention it if you don't agree with whatever they want you to do, or buy, for them. Best yet, be very careful of getting involved with Gobleers and others of that sort. If you do you will never forget it, although you will surely wish to do so.

∂

Elven Koan:
It's not the clothes that make an elf,
but the elf that makes the clothes.

Elves are also courteous in and on the Internet. Just because some Violent, or obnoxious Gobleer doesn't know who we are and can't come over and punch us out, doesn't mean we should be rude to them. That is not to say they will not find our opinions and our hard cruel truth delivered with kindness irritating, but that is another matter. Basic courtesy is always the right thing to do. Let others be rude, our trick is to endeavor to always be polite. It's a game we play. A challenge to ours'elves. And it is deliciously fun.

Also, in Internet correspondence, we find proofreading invaluable. We always proofread before we send anything. It provides greater clarity of communication and also saves us occasionally from inadvertently seeming to insult someone because we happened to leave out an essential "not" or other defining term. At the same time, we often receive letters from those who, it seems, never bother to proofread. They sound quite ignorant because of this, but we never assume that is the case. They may only be quite lazy.

And when we do receive correspondence that seems intended to insult us, we always reread it before responding. We often find that we simply misread what the person had written and jumped to conclusions about hir intention. This is a form a courtesy that has not so much to do with what we say, but with the care that we take in endeavoring to understand those who communicate with us, even those, or perhaps particularly those, who disagree with us.

However, elves consider it polite to reply to letters and emails unless the conversation has truly trailed off and there is really nothing left to say but fare thee well. In our way of thinking, those who don't reply lose the game. It is true that in some cases one must simply cease to give an incorrigible miscreant any further energy, but most of the time, even if someone is being rude to us we will still reply to them. In fact, we often enjoy responding to these letters more than any other. It gives us a chance to practice our magical powers of enchantment and courtesy.

࿆

Since we are speaking here of spiritual races, not necessarily race used to mean a genetic sub-species, but somewhat as it was use in the past, as in the French race, German race, and so forth, we elves often find we have incarnated in families that have a variety of other spiritual races in it. Most of us have relatives who may be normals, Gobleer, Grimlean, and the various associative subdivision there of, whom we often encounter in the course of our lives, as well as their friends who may be of the same type. Note that Gobleer, Grimlean and many others of this sort often like to think of themselves as normal. As always, courtesy is important in dealing with these individuals, but know that they may, and often do, judge you for being different, for being elfin or faerie. They also inevitably believe they are right and justified for doing so.

࿆

The Eldar say:
The loss of one's body is a small thing,
the loss of one's soul is everything.

207

These "normal" relatives also often wish to argue about their ideas, and it is up to you if you wish to do so, but in our opinion it is usually ill-advised to engage in such debates. These individuals are most often more passionate than reasoning. When you reach the point where their logic fails, they will either wish to stop the conversation that you didn't wish to start in the first place, or get agitated, and angry, and insist on their point of view despite all facts to the contrary. The best thing to do, we've found, besides using basic courtesy, is to always emphasize the affection you feel for them, and to accept them for who they are. They are unlikely to change, and certainly nothing we say is likely to influence them, so kind and loving understanding, without any hint of condescension, usually works well. And if it doesn't, then take comfort in the fact the family social event where you tend to encounter them will probably be over soon anyway. If they insist on arguing with you, or ranting at you, and you can't get away politely, simply listen and nod politely indicating that you understand what they are saying. If they insist on a response you can offer your opinion, but know that doing so will simply send them off on another tirade. Saying, "Well, I'll have to give that serious consideration," or "I'll have to think about that," may also serve. Best of luck on dealing with individuals such as these.

ॐ

You may also at some point encounter the Nurych. These are usually Hob-Gobleer, that is half Gobleers and half something else: elf, faerie or other, who have risen from impoverished circumstances to wealth, or are often children of those who have done so. They are eager consumers, and tend to be rather arrogant about themselves and their wealth that they assume is their divine right. At the same time, they can be rather generous with their hand-me-downs, since they buy new things often and get rid of the old periodically. If you happen to be around at the time, you may find yours'elf greatly benefited thereby. We would never have a relationship with a Nurych simply for that reason, but it is a nice bonus, yes?

And despite their prejudice, it is good to remember that Gobleer, Grimlean and others can be quite knowledgeable in their chosen field, or practice, or study. They can be expert auto mechanics, or doctors, or technicians of various sorts. It is never wise to underestimate them just because they're prejudice, and it is good to remember that despite their inflexible social leanings, there is much that an elf can learn from them. And they, like us, are also on the path of spiritual evolution, although they don't always, or perhaps seldom know or acknowledge this, and there is always that possibility that those who are behind us on the path now may surpass us somewhere further along the road that leads to enlightenment. That, at least, is something for which we can hope.

The only thing you can really
be sure of when dealing with elves is
that you never know what they'll do next.

Chapter 21:
Angels, Demons, Daemons, and Others

The word hob means half. They are halflings of various sorts, hobgoblins and various other sorts. However, the word halfling is often used to mean beings that are similar to what Tolkien called Hobbits. We elves often call these individuals the Nibblers. Nibblers are very kind for the most part and can be very hospitable, particularly when it concerns food. They like to eat and they have breakfast, sometimes pre-breakfast, second breakfast, brunch, lunch, afternoon snack or tea and biscuits, supper, dinner, or is that dinner and then supper, we are never sure, dessert, and a late night snack. They are delightful to be around usually, but for elves there is a danger of growing fat, for they eat nearly constantly, and can be a bit insulted if you don't eat with them. Even days after visiting with Nibblers these elves find ours'elves eating much more than we would usually, in a sort of gradually weaning away from over consumption. Thus, most elves must be careful of how often we visit with the Nibblers. They also love to talk and pontificate. But since we elves are good listeners, this is not a problem for us.

True victory is not to be found in winning battles, nor winning a war, but in bringing an end to the need for conflict.

We elves do our best to avoid demons and their kind, but if we do encounter them, we find that courtesy works well. It doesn't stop them from trying to trick us into some sort of one-sided deal that seems and really is too good to be true, so one must also be very firm in one's refusal to participate in any of their schemes. But again, this should be done as politely as possible, and one is advised to always treat them with respect, for they are very sensitive about being respected. Although, they do tend to confuse fear and respect, and think that people who fear them and are therefore polite to them, therefore respect them. So it is important that while treating them with respect that you do this with dignity and never, ever let them see you sweat.

☙

Daemons are genii, geniuses, and can be quite inspiring. They are your typical temperamental artist, inventor, or genius. They can be fun and interesting to know, but they can also be a pain in the ass to deal with. They tend to throw fits and tantrums, but if you can get beyond that, and not take it too seriously, they can be handled with soothing silence and transpersonal interaction. Each elf must decide if it is worth it to them to hang out with daemons, although these elves happen to love them, and have learned and benefited so very much from knowing them, despite their frequent tirades. Although, we've also found that we can only handle them for limited periods. We may hang out with them for months, or even years, but then we may take a break from them for an equal amount of time, and reconnect again later. Each elf must decide for hir own s'elf how much immature behavior sHe is willing to put up with to be inspired by a genius.

☙

It is, of course, wise to be respectful of Angels, although they are less likely to crush one to dust for disrespect as the demons and Violents are. Instead, they will simply withdraw their grace, which is to say their blessings and help from those who don't treat them with proper dignity. However, their mere presence tends to inspire awe so it is hard not to respect them, or at least shake in your boots when they are around. None-the-less, we elves treat them with respect, not merely because they are so powerful and we are but wee little things compared to them. Or simply because we are afraid they will withhold their blessings from us. They do know why someone treats them as they do and cannot be deceived on this point. We treat them with respect because that is our basic policy for treating everyone, whether they are above us or below us in power, or ahead of us or behind us on the Path of spiritual development. And it is this fact, the fact that we treat everyone with respect as much as possible, that tells the Angels that our respect for them is genuine, that it is a matter of policy with us, and not merely because they can scare the shit out of us.

We love the Pixies, particularly because these elves are also of pixie blood and disposition, which reading this book would reveal to the keen observer of Faerie life. Pixies come in many types, sizes, shapes and they have many sub-tribes. Some of these sub-tribes love to dress and live in Goth and Emo style. We are particularly fond of these folks, but they do tend to be very clannish and wary of outsiders and even if we do indicate our appreciation for them, they don't always respond. In fact, they often just withdraw or respond with a cautious nod. This doesn't bother us, however, because we love the Pixies.

Another form of the Pixies is the Piskies, often noted in our experience for pissing everywhere. They will piss out the window, in the sink, in the shrubbery and numerous other places. And they think this both clever and amusing. We had a Pisky who lived near us who continually pissed out his window. Somehow he couldn't be bothered to walk ten feet to the bathroom. And, of course, he thought it quite amusing to piss out his window. One day he told us that he kept experiencing a bad odor from outside his window. We suggested that if he stopped pissing out his window it would most certainly go away. It was as if a light bulb went on in his mind. Amazing what the power of enlightenment can do. Notice, we did not get angry with him, or scold him for being as he was, that is not the Elven Way; we merely waited until Reality collided with his fantasy and dispassionately informed him of the difference.

&

Most people have a dichotimous view of the world in which something either is real or it is not. But we elves have a paradoxical view of the world in which things can be real and unreal at the same time. It is this philosophy that allows us to move through the world that normal folk consider real and still live within the Reality of Faerie that intersects and overlaps it to function effectively in both.

Another tribe of Pixies is the Pigsies whose rooms, as the name tends to indicate, often look like pig stys. When we live with Pigsies we make sure their mess is confined to their rooms and not extended into the rest of the house. We find that is must be made very clear from the start that they cannot leave a mess in the bathroom or kitchen for others to clean up for them, which they will certainly do otherwise. Nor can they get away with telling us they will clean it up later; because they won't. Now, this goes a bit against our basic policy that if you think it should be done, do it yours'elf, but we elves are flexible folk and in dealing with Pigsies a certain discipline in the form of basic agreements is necessary. On the other hand, we don't have rules or lists of a cleaning schedule, who does the vacuuming when, etc. If the Pigsies don't want to do dishes, they don't have to, as long as they are not the dishes they dirtied. These elves are quite happy to leave them to their own creative endeavors (and Pigsies are often quite talented) as long as they clean up the mess they create in creating.

The riddle of life is death.
The riddle of death is life.
The answer to life's riddle is eternal change.
The answer to death's riddle
is everlasting bliss.

We love the Brownies. In fact, these elves are part Brownie, just as we are part Pixie. Brownies tend to love the color brown, in particular, but also will wear other earth tones. They love brown so much they often incarnate into the bodies of black people, which doesn't mean all black people are brownies, or that all brownies are black people. But if you see a black person who continually wears brown, you are probably encountering a brownie. We ran into one just the other day walking along Waikiki beach. He wore a brown aloha shirt with a slightly lighter brown flower pattern on it. Brown pants with brown Central American pattern. He had brown leather fringed moccasins on this feet, and a brown leather bag buckled around his waist, and a brown leather pill box hat on his head that had bright red fringe starting at the center in the back and extending halfway up the right side. We greeted each other warmly, immediately recognizing each other although we've never met before and we complimented him on his wondrous outfit and he commented appreciatively about the enchanter's cane with the dragon's head that Zardoa usually carries with him. We love the Brownies.

৵

We elves have no fixed limits on
how many lovers or husbands or wives a
person can have either sequentially or
if you must tread the hidden paths at night,
at least do it beneath the moon and stars.

Brownies traditionally take care of people's homes and property although, like Leprechauns, they are also noted for their shoe making skill. However, these days if they are cobblers it is usually making unique leather boots to wear at Ren Faires. They also commonly clean houses. We have often done this. Also, they love being caretakers of people's property and sometimes caregivers for the disabled. Often they will be waitresses or even housemaids in hotels or motels, until they can support thems'elves with their creative endeavors and various arts and crafts. Be kind to the Brownies. They are good, gentle folk and deserve both kindness, admiration and, as much as you can, a generous tip.

~

Sometimes you may encounter a Dull. Dulls are so boring you may wish to scream. If they are talker Dulls, you may have to politely leave. However, they may be silent Dulls who just sit there endlessly and say nothing. These we don't mind. They can sit and absorb the magic as long as they wish. Maybe it will inspire them. Be kind to the Dulls, they are actually striving to be more than they are. It is not entirely their fault they haven't achieve the level of excitement they presume they've already mastered.

~

You can often find the elves swaying or
dancing to music only they can hear.
It is the far distant sounds of Faerie
reminding us of home

Beware of Black Holes. They will suck the energy out of a room and out of your life, if you let them. They may appear harmless, they may even flatter you at first, but you will find these creatures, who are related to the Grumps, Gripes and others, are a never-ending source of danger to you or, at the very least, a pain in the posterior. They complain about everything. They are never satisfied. And they love to sue people for anything they can think of that they claim the person did that was wrong as far as they are concerned, and you can never do right as far as they are concerned. As soon as you recognize a Black Hole, politely remove yours'elf from their presence and avoid them like the plague. Never, ever, do a job for them, because you won't do it right, no matter how hard you try, and they will complain about you to everyone, at the very least, and never pay you or at least not as much as you agreed upon. You've been warned.

The elfin do not believe in the superiority of
the male over the female or the female over
the male but believe in the power of a united
people to master any quirk of fate
and of the ability of a single elf
bringing a greater light to all of us.

Chapter 22:
Ancient Lore and Customs

When we wish to move to a new area, we elves often go find the oldest, often the largest tree in the area, and speak to it, telling it of our intentions and asking for its help in entering its realm. And among the Unseelie it is often customary to present ones'elf before the Laird/Lord of a particular area before doing anything in their territory. This is also the custom, we understand, among gangs, the mafia, and other demonic groups. We Seelie Elves, on the other hand, don't have such strict divisions of territory. We are not petty Warlords. Every elf is free to come or go from our ealds as they please, as long as they do no harm when they are there. Nor do we feel an obligation to present ours'elves before others if we enter or do magic in their realms, although, if we hear of them we will often introduce ours'elves anyway. We are ever eager to make new friends and connections.

When someone insists, and we think it quite rude to do so, that we can't be elves because we don't have pointed ears, or are over three feet tall, or less than six feet tall, or that we are not blue, or albino, or some other images they have of us, we don't argue with them. Not everyone is meant to see us.

It is traditional in some countries to leave out food for elfin and faerie folk to appease us and to ask for our blessings. However, in having been educated in the possibility of salmonella, we are less inclined to accept such offerings these days. These days, if they really want to court our blessings, we suggest they take us out to dinner, or even for coffee and a scone.

৵

The ancient lore about us Faerie folk tells people not to eat or drink anything if they happen to wander into our realm, because if they do so they will not be able to leave. This is not quite true. Our food is good, wholesome, delicious and nutritious, certainly; but it is not our food that makes people wish to stay with us, but rather our courteous behavior and loving company.

৵

Some legends indicate that we elfin are insulted by an offer of payment or gifts for our services. This is not really so. We are not so easily offended, and we love accepting gifts. However, we don't like being in debt to people and if someone gives us a gift we will do our best, as soon as we can, to give them something worthy in return. We know that gifts are usually a symbol of love or affection. Although, we are also aware that sometimes they are merely given out of social custom. But we don't mind, we accept the gift as an offer of friendship and do our best to return that friendship in kind.

৵

A new day always begins in darkness.

What An Elf Would Do

We are aware that some individuals give elaborate or expensive gifts to demonstrate how wealthy, powerful, or successful they are, and often to prove they are better than someone else. This is very sad to the elves. But if they insist on giving us such gifts that we can in no way equal materially in return, we accept. What we really have to give them is an acknowledgement of their wealth and success, which is what they really want, although alas, that is a gift that even when they receive it never seems enough to them. Again, this saddens us. But all we can do is assuage their ego as best we may.

And while legends hold that we faerie folk often blind those who can see us, this is not so. On the contrary, if someone actually sees us for who we truly are, then we know that they are kin to us, of elfin blood or spirit or soul, and for us, this is always an occasion for celebration. But then, for us, nearly everything is a cause, or excuse at least, for celebration.

Also, contrary to legends, we don't kidnap babies, little kids or anyone else. It is true that when these elves had young children all the neighborhood children liked to hang around at our house, where it was more easygoing, nurturing and far less dysfunctional than theirs. They referred to our family as The Magics. But we didn't have to kidnap them to get them to hang out.
We just had to be the elves we truly are.

Chapter 23
Summoning It All Up

You may get the idea that the elves think that politeness and courtesy are the solution to every social situation and problem. This is not quite true. We know that courtesy won't transform Grimleans into less fanatical people, or persuade Gobleers to stop being greedy, or Violents not to be violent. But even in dealing with such beings courtesy is still a very good idea. While it doesn't always change a situation, although it does often soothe the way and open doors what otherwise would be closed to you, it never hurts to be polite. It is also true that there are some individuals who are scornful and suspicious of courtesy. They think we're just being smooth talkers trying to pull a fast one over on them. But that doesn't mean one shouldn't be courteous, because even these are susceptible to courtesy, particularly if it is a consistent and genuine aspect of one's behavior and character, and especially if every time you encounter these individuals you continue to treat them with respect despite their reservations. They are often won over in time. In fact, deep in their hearts, they want to be won over. Such fervent opposition always holds its opposite imprisoned within, eagerly awaiting release. And they tend to be creatures of habit, relating everything to past experience, if you are consistently polite they will eventually absorb this behavior. So be polite, be kind, be respectful always and while it won't solve every problem these are magics that will solve many problems or gain you allies among those who can solve them for you. Don't listen to those who tell you it's better to be feared than loved, or yes, listen to them politely, but don't be fooled. They are just afraid of being deceived by false courtesy. So make your courtesy consistent, not a matter of habit, but a matter of character, and the world will swayed by you as the fields of grain by the wind.

☙

If you long for love, give it.
If you yearn for beauty, create it.
If you desire wealth, share it.
Such are the secrets of the Elven Way.

About the Authors

The Silver Elves, Zardoa and Silver Flame, are a family of elves who have been living and sharing the Elven Way since 1975. They are the authors of *The Book of Elven Runes: A Passage Into Faerie; The Magical Elven Love Letters, volume 1, 2, and 3; An Elfin Book of Spirits: Evoking the Beneficent Powers of Faerie; Caressed by an Elfin Breeze: The Poems of Zardoa Silverstar; Eldafaryn: True Tales of Magic from the Lives of the Silver Elves; Arvyndase (Silverspeech): A Short Course in the Magical Language of the Silver Elves; The Elven Book of Dreams: A Magical Oracle of Faerie, Magic Talks: Being a Correspondence Between The Silver Elves and the Founders of the Elf Queen's Daughter and The Elven Book of Powers: Using the Tarot for Magical Wish Fulfillment.*

We have had various articles published in *Circle Network News Magazine* and have given out over 4,000 elven names to interested individuals in the Arvyndase language, with each elf name having a unique meaning specifically for that person. If you wish to know more about us you can read pages 100 to 107 in *Circles, Groves and Sanctuaries*, compiled by Dan and Pualine Campanelli (Llewellyn Publications, 1992), which contains an article by us and photos us and our home/sanctuary as it existed at the time. We are also mentioned numerous times in *Not In Kansas Anymore* by Christine Wicker (Harper San Francisco, 2005), and *A Field Guide to Otherkin* by Lupa (Megalithica Books, 2007).

The Elven Way is the spiritual Path of the Elves. It is not a religion. While all elves are free to pursue whatever spiritual path they desire, or not as the case may be, these elves are magicians and follow no particular religious dogma. We do however believe in all the Gods and

Goddesses, (also Santa Claus [to whom we're related], the tooth fairy [distant cousins] and the Easter or Ostara Bunny [no relation].) and try to treat them all with due respect. The Elven Way promotes the principles of Fairness, that is to say both Justice, Elegance and Equal Opportunity and Courtesy that is respectful in its interactions and attitude toward all beings, great or small. We understand the world as a magical or miraculous phenomena, and that all beings, by pursuing their own true path, will become whomever they truly desire to be. Our path is that of Love and Magic and we share our way with all sincerely interested individuals.

If you have any questions about using tarot for wish fulfillment, remember you can always contact us through our website at: http://silverelves.angelfire.com or through our Facebook page, under the name Michael Love (Silver Elves), and we will do our best to help you.

www.ingramcontent.com/pod-product-compliance
Lightning Source LLC
Chambersburg PA
CBHW070002300526
45794CB00001B/159